Stock Market Investing for Beginners

How to Make Money From Home by Trading Stocks Follow the Step-By-Step Guide and Discover WHY You NEED to Invest RIGHT NOW to Get Your First Profit in 5 Days

Adam Buffett – Warren Jones

Table of Contents

Introduction

Congratulations on purchasing *Stock Market Investing for Beginners,* and thank you for doing so.

There are different ways in which you can invest your money, but not every form of investment can help you overcome the effect of inflation. And that is where the idea of stock market investing comes in. In this book, you are going to learn everything about stock markets and how to efficiently invest your money in it to meet your goals. You will learn about how the stock market is regulated and by whom. We will also discuss the various forces at play. Once you have completed reading this book, I am sure that you can move past the jargon and see what a great opportunity the stock market provides you with.

There are numerous details that you, as a beginner, should know, and I have tried to incorporate all of it in a comprehensive yet easy-to-understand manner. I am sure none of you would want to lose your money, and so we are also going to discuss the various aspects of how you can manage your risk. I will also show you how different factors can influence the price of stocks and how you can predict a rise or fall in the market. It is not really a tough job to do once you understand the details.

There are plenty of books on this subject on the market, thanks again for choosing this one! Every effort was made to ensure it is full of as much useful information as possible, please enjoy!

Chapter 1: Important Concepts to Understand

When it comes to growing your money, one of the most common ways that people approach is through the stock market. But if you want to become an established investor, the first thing that you have to do is understand the basics, and that is exactly what we are going to discuss in this chapter. It's true that the stock market is a vast and complex network, but it is nothing that you cannot navigate with ample support and effort. Consider this chapter as a crash course to the actual word of stocks, and don't worry, I am not going to produce you a giant glossary that seems gibberish, but I am going to teach you all of it in a step-by-step manner.

What Are Stocks?

Stocks are a form of investment or specifically —
securities that will give you a portion of the company
as in you can get the ownership of a certain part of the
company — also known as shares. But what will you do
with stocks? Well, as an investor, you can buy the
stocks when you speculate that their price is going to
increase. And when the increase in price happens, you
can then sell the stocks and bring home profits.
Anyone who purchases stocks becomes the
shareholder of that particular company because they
own a part of that company. They also get to share the
profits.

Some people think that it is only the private
companies that have shareholders, but that is a wrong
concept. Both private and public companies have
stocks, and thus both of them have shareholders too.

It requires only a small group of people to form a business, but in order to get more cash for the business, companies go public and sell their stocks. This is when people buy their stocks, and they get the money. No matter how many investors have invested in the stocks, every investor will be getting their share of the profit when the company performs well. But at the same time, if the performance of the company is poor, then the investors will hold an equal risk of losing money.

The prices of stocks can swing and fluctuate all throughout the day, and there are several factors that can make it possible. We will come to those factors later. You have to realize that the stocks of all companies do not see a rise in price because some of them might not perform well after a period of time, while some can even go out of business. And in that case, investors can stand to lose a huge chunk of their money and, at times – their entire investment. That is why it is advised that you should not invest all your money in a single company. Anyways, we will talk about such strategies later in the book.

Some people own stocks without even realizing that. Do you know how? It is when you have a 401(k) because these retirement plans are often about investing the money mutual funds, which again are none other than stocks of different companies.

There are lots of risk factors associated with stock market investments, but if you look on the other hand – you also stand to gain huge profits and beat inflation. I know what you must be wondering now – how you can make money through the stock market? Well, to put it simply – there are two basic ways, and they are –

- You can earn money through dividends. These are basically regular payments that are done to the investors who bought stocks or the

4

shareholders of a company. But you have to understand that dividends are not present with all stocks, but in case your stock is providing dividends; then it is most likely to do so on a quarterly basis.

- When you buy a stock and its price increases after a certain period of time, you can make profits by selling it.

If you look at the records for the last century, the stock market has proven to give you an average return of 10% annually. But what you need to understand is the term 'average.' This percentage is calculated after considering the entire market as a whole, and it is not about any specific stock. Also, in any random year, the return will not necessarily stick to this 10% because it can be more than that or even less than that.

Demand and supply are two of the most basic factors that you need to know about if you want to get into the details about the stock market. They can greatly influence the price of stocks. When there is a huge demand for the stocks of a particular company, its prices will automatically start rising. On the other hand, when the demand falls – that is, people want to sell the shares more and not buy them – that is when the price of those shares will start going down. The concept of demand in the stock market is very much dependent on how investors see the stocks and whether they think that a particular stock has value or not.

Common Stock vs. Preferred Stock

Now, here are two terms that you should know about. Whenever you are discussing the big company stocks like Coca-Cola or Apple, it is the common stock that you are discussing. The shareholders of the common stocks have the right to attend shareholder meetings and exercise their right to vote, and they are also allowed to collect the dividends. But there is a disadvantage for common stocks as well. The common shareholders will take the hit when a company is liquidated or bankrupted as their shares are the ones that are paid at last because the preferred shareholders, bondholders, and creditors are given the first preference.

Now, in the case of preferred shares, they will not give you voting rights but will give you the dividends. And like I already mentioned above, if something were to happen to the company where it is bankrupted, and hence the stocks are liquidated, it will be the preferred shareholders who are paid first. If you ask me honestly, then I would say that you just need to care about the common stocks. This is because when you are investing in say a very large company; it is quite unlikely that they will go bankrupt in the near future. So, you don't have to panic so much about the loss of value in common shares. It is usually the more complex investors who deal with preferred shares.

What Are Stock Exchanges?

The next important thing that you have to learn in relation to stocks is the stock exchanges. This is basically a platform where the trading of stocks takes place. The sellers and buyers of the stock market connect with each other at the stock exchange.

There are different stock exchanges, and every stock that is there is there in the market belongs to one of these stock exchanges—for example, the NYSE or New York Stock Exchange and the Nasdaq. If a company wants their stocks to be traded on these exchanges, there are certain requirements that they have to meet, first requirement is that every share they list should be at least $4 in price. The companies which are more related to the technology industry are available on Nasdaq, and the larger companies are on the NYSE. Well, the exchange on which a stock is being traded is not very crucial. You should not build a mindset where you dislike a stock just because it is traded at some particular exchange you don't like.

But there is one exception to this, and they are OTC exchanges or over-the-counter exchanges. Here you will find the 'pink sheet stocks.' These stocks belong to speculative companies, and these stocks don't have to report their quarterly earnings mandatorily. Their trading volume is quite low, and you might even see regular swings. Moreover, they don't have to be registered with the SEC or the Securities and Exchange Commission. If you look carefully, you will also find certain companies on these OTC exchanges that were barred from the larger exchanges like Nasdaq for some reason. I am not saying that all stocks on these exchanges are bad, but nonetheless, you should be very careful before getting involved with them and do your research well.

But you don't have to worry so much because I'm sure almost every stock that you are going to name is either listed on NYSE or Nasdaq, and they are not present on any OTC exchange. Also, you don't really have to know about the exchange on which any particular stock is listed in order to trade. Your broker will simply trade the shares if you ask them to.

Some people often get confused between indexes and exchanges. Well, they are completely different. In simpler terms, the stocks are sold and bought on exchanges, but the indexes basically are a representation of a particular theme, and they are a collection of all the stocks that fall under that categorization criterion. We will discuss more on indexes in the next section.

What Are Stock Indexes?

Let me give you an example, and it will make it easier for you to understand the whole thing. The S&P 500 is probably the most popular indexes, and everyone in the stock market knows about it. It is basically a collection of 500 U.S. companies that are publicly-traded and are also the largest in the country. Some companies included in this list are PayPal, Kohl's, Amgen, and so on. Then there is the Russell 2000, which is another index, and it specifically lists a total of 2000 small stocks.

When an investor wants to understand a specific market or measure it, they use indexes of that specific market. Let us say you want to understand the performance of the small-cap stocks; then, you will have to check the Russell 2000. Every index has its own methodology of calculation. But one thing that you have to understand is that these indexes are considered to be the benchmark in their respective fields. For example, the S&P 500 is the index that is used by most mutual fund companies to check whether their returns are at par with the market.

What Is an IPO?

This is another term that you are going to come across quite frequently if you are to stay in the stock market and so I want to clarify it right in the beginning. IPO is the acronym for an Initial Public Offering, and it is basically the event when a company decides to become public or produce its shares in the open market for making them available to everyone for purchase. Now, you might be wondering why a company would do that – well, there are several reasons and not just one. But the major reason why people do that is that they want to raise more money for their business. When an IPO is conducted, the company sells its shares and, thus, brings in more money. It definitely is an extensive process, and there are two major reasons why people tend to get excited about an IPO.

The first reason is simple – it is because the company is making its shares public for the first time. Let me give you an example, in 2012, Facebook went public for the first time and investors were very excited about it because they believed in the company and now they can finally have some of it as their own. The second reason is that the investors want to analyze the movement of the stocks of the company on the day it becomes public. The higher the investor excitement, the more upward movement you will see. In fact, in 2004, when the stocks of Google had been made public, on the first day, the prices had risen by 18%. Another astonishing example was that of LinkedIn – on the day of its IPO, the prices rose by more than 100%.

Now, I know that after reading through all this stuff, you probably think that IPOs are all very fun, exciting and good to invest in, but there is another picture that you don't know about – IPOs are driven by emotions and are often erratic. So, they don't really serve as the optimum investment time. Moreover, if you do a little bit of digging, you will also find that in most cases,

IPOs want to draw in more investors, and that is why they are underpriced. This benefits the company by increasing its first-day gains. If you want to watch what happens, IPOs can be fun, but if you are looking forward to investing, then I would suggest that you will get better places for your money.

Who Is a Stockbroker?

Lastly, you need to understand who a stockbroker is and what are their duties? Usually, there are two things that this term can mean. Firstly, it can be referring to some person who is responsible for guiding you in the right direction with regards to your trade. They can even help you manage your capital in a better way and give you advice on market movements. They can even trade on your behalf, and you simply have to pay them a fee. So, in short, your stockbroker is a person who is your investment advisor. In order to be a stockbroker, the person has to give licensing exams and pass through a training that is quite extensive. They have immensely vast market knowledge.

But most of the time, when we are talking about a stockbroker, it does not refer to any single person but rather a company or to be more specific – a brokerage firm. This company would then be responsible for placing your trades.

How Is Stock Price Determined?

Now that we have covered the basics about the stock market, it is time we look into some of the finer details like how are the stock prices determined. Stock prices go up and down all the time, but do you know why? If you want to pinpoint the exact reason behind the price of a stock, then I am telling you this right now – it is impossible. There are not one but plenty of factors acting behind the price of a single stock, and it is not influenced singularly by any of them. But yes, with a little effort, you can easily understand the basics behind the price determination of stocks.

Before that, let me give you a brief intro into the capital markets –

- **Primary markets** are set up by the capital markets so that a company is able to raise money through an IPO. An initial price is set up after consulting the investment bankers, and then investors start lining up for the stocks of that company.

- Now that the IPO is done, the stocks have been bought by the common investors who can then, in turn, buy or sell them in the **secondary market**. This happens in different stock exchanges. Now, here the price is influenced by demand and supply. The ultimate price of the shares will be decided by the bid and ask price. The ask price is referred to as the minimum price that the seller will accept to get the concerned security. The bid price is the highest price that the buyers are ready to pay for purchasing the concerned shares.

Some other factors that should be factored in when you are discussing the price or when the price is determined are as follows –

- The first factor is the earnings of the company in question. I will agree that the stock price is definitely not influenced on a daily basis by this factor, but before any investment decisions are finalized, the earnings of the company are something that will be looked into by analysts.
- Institutional investors and the trades they perform is the second factor that you should have a look at. Hedge funds, mutual funds, or even pension plans might be included in this.
- Thirdly, the market conditions definitely influence the price of stocks. Let us say; there is some bad or good market event, then it can

directly influence the price of the stocks as well. For example, in 2008, when there was a financial crisis, there was a drop of 37% in the S&P 500.

How to Read Stock Quotes?

Stock quotes can seem hard to read, not only to a beginner but even for a seasoned trader. There is a combination of numbers that you have to figure out. The different elements that are present in a stock quote have been explained below and once you know them, reading a stock quote should become easier –

- **Company Name** – If you see a stock table, you will notice that there are so many shares, and all of them have to be fitted in that space, so no company uses its full name. To get over this space crunch, companies have specific symbols, and you have to know them. You can search them on the internet or the trading platform of your broker.

- **Stock Price –** This is quite obvious that your stock quote will include the stock price. The price basically keeps fluctuating not only on a daily basis but also every minute. They remain constant only when the markets have been closed.

- **High/Low –** With time, as more and more trades are conducted, the live share prices keep fluctuating. The valuation of a stock decreases when it is sold, and it increases when it is bought. Thus, the price of a share is affected accordingly. So, the stock quote makes it easier for an investor to compare, and because of that, both the lowest and highest price hit by the stock on that particular day is mentioned in the stock quote.

- **Close –** When the market closes, the stock prices also stop changing. So, the close here refers to the closing price, and so it will tell you about the last price at which the stock was traded on that day. If you look at this particular value when the market is open, you will be looking at the closing price for the previous day.

- **Net Change –** Since the stock quote mentions the closing price, you can imagine how easy it becomes to automatically calculate the change in price that took place. Both an absolute value and a change of percentage is mentioned when this change is stated. If there has been an increase in the price of a stock from what it was the previous day, then it is a positive change and vice-versa. The color green is used to mark a positive change, whereas a negative change is indicated by the color red.

- **52-Week High/Low –** Here, the number 52 refers to the 52 weeks in a year or simply one year, and this will represent the lowest and highest prices of that stock in one year. The investor will then be able to find out how the stock has performed over a broader time period.

- **Dividend Details** – As you already know, for the investors, dividends serve as the primary income source, and for anyone who is in the market for the long-term, this information is valuable. That is why the dividend yield is something that you will find mentioned in certain stock quotes.

- **PE Ratio** – When the price of the stock of the company is divided by the earnings per share, you get the PE ratio and the market sentiment is what dictates this ratio. You will often get it in the stock quotes.

- **Volume** – Lastly, the demand for the stocks dictates the volume of trade of the stocks of a particular company. This section will show you exactly how many stocks of the company have changed hands.

Chapter 2: Getting Into the Mindset of a Stock Trader

Now, I know what you must be thinking – why is psychology so important when it comes to the stock market when we are dealing with numbers and finance? Well, what you have to understand is that you can only be successful in the stock market when you are confident and not overtaken by greed or fear. You have to learn how to contain both these emotions, and only then you can make good profits. If you let your emotions come in the way, then you will not be able to form an unbiased analysis of the market fundamentals. Exercise disciplinary skills, quick thinking, and controlling your emotions are some of the things that you have to learn to master.

Tips to Think and Act Like a Stock Trader

Yes, I agree that qualitative analysis can help you understand a lot when it comes to the stock market, but at the same time, it will only get you up to a certain extent. After that, you have to adopt the trader's mindset if you want to make handsome profits. Here are some tips that you can follow in order to do so –

Don't Panic

Panic will be your worst enemy, so try to avoid it as much as possible. In fact, if you cannot keep it together, you might take some irrational decisions just because you let panic take over you. That is why people end up buying stocks when they shouldn't have or selling stocks when they should have held them for a bit longer.

24

When things take the wrong term, it is quite normal for you to panic, and I am not saying that it is abnormal if you do. But what I am telling you to do is that you should learn to keep your panic under control. It is your choice what you want to do with your panic. Do you want to let it control you, or are you willing to harness the energy from your panic to motivate yourself to do better? You can move up a rung in the ladder of competition if you start doing some more research and get to know the details of the market even better. If you want to become better, you can use this strategy instead of panicking.

Also, if you have a really bad situation ahead of you, I know that your first instinct might be to act on it, but you have to control it and think before you act. Sometimes, your thoughts will start becoming clearer and more logical if you step back and take a minute before making any huge investment decision.

Understand the Concept of Fear

Once you understand how fear works in the case of the stock market, mitigating risks and making profits would become a bit easier than before. Whenever there is some bad news about the economy of any company in specific, the first reaction is that traders get scared. Some people think that they should be liquidating their stocks at once, and this kind of overreacting is because they let their fear take over them. They think that if they take their cash out and sit on it, they will be protecting themselves from overexposing to too much risk. Now, in such cases, it might happen that their decision was right, and this saved them from significant losses, but it can also happen that in doing so, they skipped an opportunity of profit, which arose shortly after they left the market.

Whenever the body thinks that there is a perceived threat, fear is what your mind responds with, and this is totally normal. But you have to learn how you can quantify your fear. Think deeply and find out what it is exactly that you fear and also be specific about why you fear it. When you are well-researched about the market, you think ahead of time, and this will help you in staying prepared for anything that comes your way. If you want to maintain a good portfolio, this is necessary. I am not saying this will be easy, but it is of utmost importance.

You Must Have a Fallback Position

You should always keep your fallback position ready in your mind when you are investing in the stock market. For example, it can be a certain percentage of the amount you invested. If you notice that the price of a stock has reduced to 15% below the amount that you had initially invested, you can choose to liquidate or sell your shares.

Let us say that you have purchased stocks in a car company, and now you are coming to know that the prices of fuel might rise, and this means that the car companies are going to be negatively affected. So, you have to figure out a way in which you can hedge the risk. For example, you can go and choose to purchase some shares in a company that belongs to the domestic oil industry. So, the idea is that you should always have a position ready that will help you mitigate the risks that are coming your way.

Overcome Greed

If you want to be a successful trader, you have to fight off greed. If you think that you cannot really get greedy because you know it will be risky, let me tell you something. Every trader has become greedy at some point in their life or the other. Suppose you know your trades are winning, but you want to make more profits, so you hold on to the position for a bit longer only to find that there is a steep fall in the price. This is not some made-up story, this is reality, and it happens all the time. So, if you think that holding on to your trade will make you more profits, then you are wrong. The trades can go in the other direction at any time, and your greediness will incur you huge losses.

It will not be an easy task to overcome the feeling of greed. This is because greed comes from a human instinct where they want to stick to the plan a bit more because they think they will do better. So, you see? In order to get rid of greed, you will have to close the trade instead of waiting. Greed is an instinct that has to be identified at the right time. That is also why you should have a trading plan in place so that you do not act whimsically and go by the book. You can set stop loss points, as explained above. You will stop your trade whenever these points are reached. Similarly, you can also set a profit target, which, when reached, you will exit from the trade. There is another method you can implement. You can set a daily limit as to the amount of money you are willing to, and you can afford to lose on any particular day.

Important Traits Found In a Successful Trader

Most beginners have the same question in mind —
what makes a successful trader? Well, I don't think it is
that easy to answer your question because there are a
number of traits that you should possess if you want to
be successful in the world of stocks. Trading or
investing in the stock market is not all about strategies
because there is a lot more than that. The traits that
you develop are the reason behind you successfully
implementing all the strategies. You might be having
one, two, three, or even more traits from the list, but
remember that if you truly want to succeed, you have
to inculcate all the traits and not just some. If you think
of it the other way, you will realize that no one is born
with the talent of making money in the stock market, it
is a process, and everyone learns as they go.

So, here are some of the traits that you should work on
—

Optimistic Attitude

If you are a pessimist or someone who goes into a negative cycle of thinking very easily, then I am sorry to say, but investing in the stock market is not for you. A healthy dose of optimism can even be called as the important pre-requisite of a trader. Do you know why? Well, if you are not positive, then all that negativity will eventually lead you to take rash decisions. You have to believe in yourself and your skills that no matter how much losses you have incurred or how bad the market condition is, you always have it in yourself to find yourself back and build back the profits.

There is another thing that you have to understand, and that is – trading is a zero-sum game, and there are two teams – winners and losers. What you have to do is always visualize yourself on the winning team.

Discipline

The next most important trait that you should possess is discipline. If you think that you are having a bad time in the market, don't worry, you are going to get countless possibilities to make up for your loss. If you perform a bunch of successful trades, then there is a possibility that you might mess them up every other second. You might skip successful trades or trade more than you should increase your exposure to risk. No matter how much active of a trader you are, if you think carefully, then you will notice that the actual trading time for any person during the day is really short. So, what do you do in the other part of the day? You stay disciplined so that you do not end up making any bad decisions. You wait for any signal to arise so that you can go forward with your strategy, but make sure you don't go off your trading plan.

Being disciplined means that when the market is not producing you with many opportunities, you sit still and don't do anything irrational. Similarly, if you are disciplined, you act in the right way when the market does provide you an opportunity, and you have to act instantaneously. When you are in the trade, staying disciplined means that you will act according to your trading plan and not go rogue with your strategies.

Ability to Learn From Your Mistakes

We will be discussing the common mistakes made by traders and investors in the last chapter of this book, but what I want to tell you now is that no matter how many mistakes you make, the main lesson is that you have to learn from them. Every successful trader or investor that you see today has undergone an extensive learning process before they could reach where they are today, and the same applies to you too. You have to prepare yourself to adopt this learning mentality and keep learning throughout your life. Just because you made some successful trades successively doesn't mean that you know everything.

33

There are always things left to learn, and so, you should have an open mind about learning.

In fact, I can tell you that the mistakes you make are your greatest learning tool. One of the ways in which you can learn from your mistakes is if you maintain a journal or any such kind of record about your trades and the actions you take and whether they were successful or not. You have to review your own behaviors and actions because no one else is going to do that for you. You have to clear your mind, and you have to assess your own behaviors carefully. There should be a continual development plan, and for that, you have to keep a close eye on your growth.

Patience

Remember how we discussed the trait of discipline? Well, patience is somewhat related to it, but I still want to discuss it separately because there are things that you should know. If you are into something like day trading where buying and selling are done on the same

34

day, you have to have a lot of patience. Similarly, if you are investing in stocks, you need patience too. For trading, you have to identify when it is time to exit the market. If you leave too early just because you fear that you will be losing money, you might miss an opportunity for handsome gains.

I have met so many traders whose main problem is that they do not have the patience that is required to wait for that correct entry and exit points. The stock market is all about split seconds of action and then prolonged waiting periods. You have to undergo this see-saw if you want to bring home good profits.

Adaptability

The last trait that I am going to talk about is adaptability. Once you are in the stock market for a considerable period of time, you will notice that no two days are going to be alike. So, if you are someone who is stuck only to the textbook examples, you are going to have a hard time in the real world. There is a whole world of difference between when you read a strategy and when you implement it in the current market conditions.

Those who are successful can deal with all types of market conditions and yet implement their strategies confidently, and that is exactly what you have to do. For that, you need to be adaptable. You need to build mental flexibility because no two days are going to be the same.

How to Determine the Right Time to Buy or Sell?

If only you had something that would have informed you of whether the stock prices are going to rise or fall, investing in the stock market would have become so much easier, right? There would be nothing stopping your portfolio from growing. There is something called the RSI or the Relative Strength Index with which you can figure out whether the price of any stock has reached a point of reversal or not, but there are certain disadvantages of this tool as well. It is not a tool that you can use for all investments, and if you want to figure out the right time to buy or sell stocks, read on to find out more.

Understand the Cycle of Shareholding

The shares constantly keep fluctuating between being oversold and overbought. These are some predictable cycles that every company goes through, no matter how good they are. Even if they had a continuous phase of success, this cycle of shareholding is inevitable. But what is important here is that you can actually check whether a stock has been oversold or overbought within a matter of a few seconds. And you have to understand that these conditions are not permanent and they will get reversed soon. When stocks are overbought, their prices fall, and when they are oversold, their prices rise. The goal of every market is to return itself to a normal state.

There is a point of peak and decline for every stock. Let us say that a very famous company has been doing well in the market and is driving higher prices. The investors will then jump into the shares of the company, which results in the stocks being overbought. In such a situation, the prices start climbing, and soon they reach a mark where the prices become too exorbitant for the buyer.

Now, let us see what happens in the reverse condition. When prices rise to such a level, the buyers start believing that there will be a drop, and so that is when a massive selling of shares starts. That is how the condition of being oversold results. If anyone has their shares still in hand, they do not sell it because they know selling it would mean losing a large chunk of the money. So here is what you learned in this section –

- There will be a fall in the price of overbought shares

- There will be a rise in the price of oversold shares

If you want to know the extent to which a stock is oversold or overbought, you can do so with the help of several online portals, and then you can decide for yourself whether there will be a rise in price or a fall.

Use the RSI

This is basically a technical indicator that is widely used, and the value of RSI can be anything between 0 and 100. If the level of RSI is below 30, then you have to understand that the stock is oversold. Also, if the level of RSI is over 70, then the conclusion is that the stock is overbought. The RSI is quite like the elastic band in real life. Do you know why? It's because the further it moves in either direction that is 0 or 100, the other direction will pull at it even harder. That is also the reason why you won't see to many RSIs that are below 20 or above 80.

Learn About Market Resistance

This is another concept that you have to learn if you want to know how you can determine the exact time of buying or selling stocks. When a stock is overbought, there will come the point that acts as a tipping point where demand in the market is almost nil, and the investments start to slide. Similarly, there is also a point at which the investments begin to rise because of the inflow of demand once again. Well, if you see it that way, the RSI is also a measure of this same concept of support and resistance in the market.

Market resistance is when the high prices of stocks can no longer be supported by the market, and so the price is pushed back down. Market support keeps rising when demand is present in enough quantities to prevent a fall in price.

Identify Opportunities That Are Undervalued

If you want to figure out whether stocks are undervalued or not, start by examining the prospect of growth in the company's assets in the near future.

The DCF analysis or the Discounted Cash Flow analysis is going to help you out in this respect. The cash flow of the company in the future is considered, and then a reasonable risk factor is chosen to discount that flow back to the present. The theoretical price target is calculated by summing up all the discounted cash flows. Now, a stock will be considered to be good to purchase when the current stock price is less than this value. You should also consider looking at stocks that have their RSI values less than 30. It is important that you put your focus on the bigger picture because stocks are eventually going to return to a condition of being oversold.

Chapter 3: Investing in the Stock Market

Investing in the stock market is something that everybody should learn because it will help you to beat inflation. It doesn't matter how little money you have; once you have figured out basic things like repaying all your debts and constructing an emergency fund, you should start to invest in the stock market with as little as you can. But before you commit to anything, you have to learn the process, and that is exactly what we are going to discuss in this chapter.

How to Invest in the Stock Market?

The stock market can definitely be your money-making machine if you do things right. But first, let me explain you the procedure that is followed for making any investments in the stock market.

Step 1 – Determine Your Financial Goals

Before you put a single penny in stocks, you have to figure why you want to do this and what your investment goals are. You also have to perform an honest assessment of your current financial situation so that you can be sure that you are at a place to accommodate this new activity. Some things that you should take into your consideration are as follows –

- Assess whether you are going to have a stable income for the coming months or even years.
- If you have any heavy debts, consider clearing them first before taking any new endeavor.
- If you have any big family responsibility on your shoulders, like marriage or a newborn in the house, figure out whether you have enough money to cover that.

- Lastly, take your monthly household budget into consideration before you decide how much money you want to put aside for stocks.

After answering all the things that I just mentioned above, your task is to think about what your goals are – do you want to buy a house? Are you saving for retirement? Do you want to support your child's schooling? When we are talking about financial goals for the stock market, it is better if they are for the long-term because, in the short-term, the risk of losing your money is much more.

Step 2 – Open a Retirement Account

If you are a beginner in stock market investing, then I would suggest that you start your journey by opening a retirement account like the 401(k) plan or any other equivalent of it. In case there is no employer plan, then you can also go with the IRA or Individual Retirement Account. These accounts are not only tax-sheltered, but they are also allowing you to invest your money in the stock market until you are ready to do so directly.

Step 3 – Choose a Stockbroker

When you think you are ready to invest in the stock market on your own, the first thing to do is choose an online broker to suit your needs and also your budget because some of them might be giving you a lot of features, but they also charge hefty commissions. For starters, you have to understand that there are two types of stockbrokers –

- The first type is the full-service brokers who charge more commissions, but they are also quite comprehensive, and they provide you with tailor-made strategies. Investors who have enough capital go with these because they get extensively researched advice and also huge resources at their disposal.
- The next type of brokers which most people use are discount brokers because their services

46

are quite affordable, and you will be getting a platform to conduct the trades even though it is not as extensive as the ones provided by full-service brokers.

Step 4 – Begin With Mutual Funds

I usually advise the beginners to start investing with mutual funds because you don't have to worry about anything with these funds. There are professional fund managers who will work on mitigating the risks and also encourage good performance by implementing necessary strategies. You basically don't have to do any of those things, and the only thing that you have to do is figure out how much money you want to invest in these funds. One of the best things about mutual funds is that they are already diversified, and so all your eggs are never in one basket.

Step 5 – Invest in Index Funds

If you want to make the process a bit more hassle-free, then I would suggest you start investing in index funds.

47

I already explained what the S&P 500 index means and suppose you invest in an index fund that follows the S&P 500, then the performance of your investment will follow it precisely. It is true that when you invest in an index fund, you don't have chances of over-performing it, but at the same time, you don't have chances of under-performing it either.

Step 6 – Use Dollar-Cost Averaging Method

This is basically a process by which you don't get into any investment at once but rather gradually. For example, instead of investing an entire amount of $2000 in one index fund, you can make say $200 investment every month for a period of ten months. By this process, you will never be buying at the top of the market, and instead, you buy at different times.

Step 7 – Educate Yourself About Investments

There is no end to how much you can learn about the stock market, and you should not ever stop learning. When you open an account with your broker, you are going to access to lots of resources on the platform itself, but even after that, you should look into different major financial magazines, buy books, and listen to podcasts to develop your trading psychology and know about all the latest strategies. You can also try paper trading where you will get the perfect opportunity to test your trading skills without losing any money so that with time, you are totally prepared to face the real world.

Step 8 – Go Into Direct Stock Investments Gradually

Do you know why I asked you to open a retirement account or start with mutual funds and index funds? It is because I want you to get yourself used to the market environment first. This is a gradual process. If you dive into the stock market right away, you probably don't know anything, and the chances are that you will be losing all your money. But with gradual exposure, you will learn a thing or two every day and polish your skills in the process.

Step 9 – Monitor Your Portfolio

Once you start investing, you cannot simply put your money in one stock and never look at it. You have to monitor your portfolio constantly. You have to understand that the stock market is highly dynamic, and it will keep changing every minute. If you are not aware of what is going on, you may as well wake up one day to find that all your capital is lost. But yes, I am not asking you to react to every rise or fall in price. But you should keep your research alive and wait patiently. If you notice any changes that might have a grave impact on your portfolio, you have to do some damage control.

Step 10 – Always Diversify!

If you have followed all the steps in the same order as I told you to, then your portfolio is already diversified by the time you reach the final step. But even after that, when you are investing in stocks directly, don't invest all your money in a single place. You should put some of your money in growth funds, some of it in bonds, and some in international funds. This will ensure that even if something happens in one of the funds, your money in other funds is safe.

How to Make Money in the Stock Market?

In the previous section, I already told you the step-by-step process of starting your investments in the stock market. In this section, I am going to give you some advice on how you can make money while following those steps.

Take Full Advantage of Time

There are ways in which you can make money in the stock market even though you are there for the short-term, but the real benefit of the stock market is its compounding effect, and that can only happen in the long run. The money that is present in your account will grow as the value of the assets keep increasing. This means that you are going to receive even more capital gains. So, with time, there is an exponential increase in the value of stocks.

But if you really want this exponential factor to work in your favor, your investments in the stock market should start as early in your life as possible. So, the ideal way would be to start investing the moment you start earning, no matter how much it is. Like I told you in the previous section, look for a 401(k) plan that is company-sponsored.

An example should make it clearer to you as to what I am trying to explain. Let us say that you had put $1000 in your retirement account when you were of the age of 20. So, if you continue to work until the next 50 years, that is the age 70, and let us say that you did not put anything else into your retirement account. Even then, you will get something around $18,000 at the end of the term, assuming that there was a 6% rate of interest, which is quite moderate. But let us say that you made the initial deposit of $1000 60 years later, then you would be having only $800 in your account. So, you will be able to take full benefit of the power of compound interest only when you start your investment early.

Practice Investing Regularly

In the above paragraph, I already showed you how important time is when it comes to stock market investments, but time is not the only factor working here. If you decide not to save anything or anything reasonable, then even a decade of time couldn't turn your money into a handsome amount.

I will use the previous example again. Let us say that instead of a one-time investment of $1000, you decide to contribute $1000 every year. And if you divide it, you will see that you have to save $20 each week to save $1000 in a year, and I think $20 is something which is pretty easy to save. Now, let's assume that you start making the deposits when you are 20. Then, on your 70th birthday, you will be having $325,000 in your bank account. But instead of doing that, if you started saving from when you were 60 but invested a $1000 every year, you'd have something around $15,000 in your account.

In fact, if you have a regular source of income, then you don't have to think about the payments – you can simply automate them, and they will be made on time. You can set a particular payment amount every week or every month.

Maintain a Portfolio That Is Diverse

Diversification is the key to making good profits in the market. There is a risk associated with every type of investment that you do. Sometimes, the companies that you are investing in now might be underperforming in the course of one year. But that is where diversification comes into play. If you don't invest all your money in one place, you will be safeguarding it against aspects that come out of the blue or are unplanned.

It is highly unlikely that when something happens, for example, a geopolitical event, all the stocks will be equally suffering. There will always be some stocks that are performing well while there will be others that are not performing that well. But if you have diversified your portfolio, then you will have better chances at hedging and mitigating the risk.

Take the Help of Some Professional

If you are a beginner, you should consider taking some professional help so that once you learn and you in on the trade, you can do everything by yourself. But before that, trading platforms can help you do all the research so that you are not wasting any of your time on that. It is true that your chances of loss cannot be mitigated even when you are using professional help, but when you have an expert working with you, you will automatically feel better and secure.

How to Succeed in the Stock Market?

If you want to be a successful investor, you have to understand that there is no shortcut to that – you simply have to give more effort. If you are someone who is following the feelings that your gut tells you, that is not how you can be successful. In fact, that is how you are going to lose a lot of money. If you had guessed something and it turned out to be right, then you cannot call that a win. It was simply a coincidence. In order to succeed, you have to design full-proof strategies and also execute them in the right manner. Just like in a game of football, the team does not enter the field without a strategy; similarly, if you want to win in the stock market, don't set foot if you have not devised your strategy yet.

Choose a Strategy After Figuring Out Your Goals

This is something very important that you should keep in mind. I know it might sound like a cliché, but your strategy will never be the right one for you until and unless you align it with your goals. You have to know where you want to go in life, and only then you can drive yourself up to that point. The goal that you set has to be highly focused and very specific. For example, 'I want an early retirement and possibly at the age of 40 so that I still have enough time to start something new'. This is not a specific goal. This has a lot of vague terms. You can fix a goal that looks like this – 'I want to retire by the age of 40, and I want to accumulate at least $250,000 apart from the 401(k) plan. At the age of 45, I want to increase it to $350,000 so that I can start my own line of home décor products.' This is something highly specific. I am not saying to apply these same numbers to yourself. You can wish for something entirely different. But whatever it is, make sure it is specific.

In the next section, I am going to discuss the major investing approaches that you should know about in

order to succeed in the stock market, and they are –
value, growth, and blended.

Value Investing

When it comes to long-term, it is value investing that is
going to give you the maximum returns, but it is also
the one that is most difficult. For value investing, your
task would be to look for companies that are listed on
the exchange at prices that is quite below the true
market value of that company. It might be that the
sector in which the company lies is not something
people are seeking right now, or it might also be that
the company has run out of favor. Analyzing the
candidates is the most difficult part of value investing.

You have to analyze the financials diligently, and if you
are right about the company, then the payoff will be
handsome. Once the stocks of the company have
been rediscovered by people, the price will then be
raised to a much higher level. But for this to happen,

you might have to hold on to the stock for quite a long time.

Growth Investing

The next type that we are going to discuss is growth investing, and it is the part that everyone is so excited about. In simpler terms, you have to analyze and find companies whose growth potential in the near future is huge. But make sure you don't choose the shooting stars. This means you should steer clear of the companies that show themselves in the market only for a short period of time, and then they are never heard of. You have to look for companies that have a solid base and will also prove good for your business.

When people become too much focused on the small-cap stocks, that is when growth investing becomes risky. It is true that small-cap stocks are the ones that have a lot of potential for rapid growth, but when it comes to success in the long-term, they face a lot of odds too. You will get plenty of large-cap stocks that are currently in a position where they show strong potential for growth in the future.

Blended Investing

The next form, as you might have understood from the name, is a balance between growth and value investing. You will be able to achieve proper asset allocation if you can strike a balance between the two. The potential risk or return involved can be decreased or increased by adjusting the mix of the assets. Your strategy should also be in line with your time frame and your goals.

When you are devising your investment strategy, do you know what the most important factor is? It is your risk tolerance. So, weight in all the factors and choose the one that suits you the best.

Best Point of Entry and Exit

In this section, we are going to discuss what entry and exit points are, and then I will explain to you how you can identify them.

Entry Point Definition

When you are trading, the price at which you try to sell or buy a security is called the entry point. It should basically be included in your trading strategy so that you can eliminate all types of emotions from the trade and think logically.

When you want to start trading, you first have to make a transaction that involved either selling or buying. Let us say you have identified a stock that seems attractive to you, and you think that the stock is overpriced. Now, you wait for the price to decrease to a certain level, and then you decide to buy it. This is the point where you enter the transaction, and so the price at which you purchase the stock is referred to as the entry point. If

61

you want your returns to be maximized, you have to determine both the entry point and the exit point prior to the trade and make sure there is a sufficient gap between both so that there is sufficient growth of your portfolio.

Determining Entry Points

If there has been a counter-trend move in the market, then you can expect the arrival of a good entry point. There are several indicators like the trending moving averages that you can use to figure out these entry points. You can find the resistance and support areas on the stock charts if you connect the peaks and troughs with the help of the trendlines. The support trendline is where you are probably going to find a good entry point, and this will be for a long trade. If you are looking for a short trade entry point, then you should look close to the resistance trendline.

Exit Point Definition

The price at which you (as a trader or investor) want to close your position is termed as the exit point. If you want to exit your trade as an investor, you sell your assets. But for a trader, he may either sell or buy in order to exit. Depending on the price movement, the exit point can either bring your profits or a loss. Based on the expectations that a particular investor or trader has and their risk tolerance, the exit points keep varying. In general, the trade will be for a longer-term when the exit point is far from the entry point.

Determining Exit Points

Just like the entry point, the exit point is of equal significance because you definitely wouldn't want to leave the market too early or too late. So, if you want to know when it is the right time to exit a trade and call it a night, you can use trendlines to figure out your exit point. Let us say that the trade was going on all well, but before it could reach the trendline support, the stock closed. Such a situation suggests that the trend has already finished its course, and your duty would be to lock any gains that you have made so far.

In order to lock the gains and mitigate risks, exit points are planned out from way ahead. If you have come this far in the book, then you already know that it is easy to buy and sell stocks, but reading the trendlines and performing technical analysis is a whole new thing. Once you have grasped the concept of these chart patterns, identifying exit and entry points that hold potential will become way easier.

Chapter 4: Fundamental Approaches in Stock Investing

In the previous chapter, I had given you a basic introduction to both value investing and growth investing, and in this chapter, we are going to explore these topics in greater detail.

Growth Investing

As you must have understood from the term, in the case of growth investing, the focus is on multiplying the capital of the investor, and the strategies are devised accordingly. These investors put their money in the growth stocks. Now, growth stocks basically comprise of companies that are small or young or, in

65

simpler words, companies who have the potential to grow their earnings in the near future, and the rate of the increase should be above the average when compared with the overall market condition.

This kind of investing can be really attractive, and several investors pursue it because of the impressive returns involved. But those returns depend entirely on the success of the companies. At the same time, a fairly large amount of risk is also involved in this approach because the companies that are present in the growth stocks are usually untried. The five key factors that have to be looked into for approaching growth investing are as follows – returns on equity, profit margins, future and historical growth in earnings, and the performance of the share price. The main idea behind growth investing is to increase the capital either through short-term or long-term capital appreciation.

In typical scenarios, all the industries that are rapidly increasing are under the radar of growth investors. They sometimes even examine entire markets. They focus on capital appreciation, so instead of relying on dividends, they focus on the profits they are getting from selling their stocks. You should also know, in most cases, the earnings are reinvested by the growth-stock companies into their own business, and they do not pay dividends. The idea behind growth investing is that since these companies are new and small, they have a lot of potential in them to expand. Another term that is used to refer to growth investing is capital appreciation strategy because of one single reason – this strategy is all about focusing and maximizing the capital gains.

Traits You Should Look For in Growth Stocks

In this section, we are going to talk about certain traits that will help you understand which are the best growth stocks to invest in –

- **Impressive Market Opportunity** – A growth of 10% in revenues every year is something that is supposed to be present in growth stocks in order to categorize them as successful. And this is something that is almost not possible unless and until there is some great market opportunity that the company pursued. In usual cases, a company can be called a growth company if it has become a major name in its specific niche, and the industry that it is in should be promising too. With time, the company should be able to expand its reach into markets that are adjacent to it so that the overall reach can be broadened. When the company increases itself into those new markets, the direct result is that the revenue starts increasing, and in this way, it paves the way for its future growth.

- **Competitive Advantage in the Long-Term** – This is another important point that should be kept in mind when it comes to growth investing. Every company has its competitors, but the advantage over the competitors should be maintained over the long-term in order to reap any benefits from it. The growth can be sustained only in this way. The main types of competitive advantage have been discussed below for your ease –

- For a business with an online marketplace, network effects have to be taken under consideration, especially when the value of the business increases.
- Greater retention of customers can be established by increasing the switching costs so that the existing customers think twice before going to the rival companies.
- A flexible pricing system is usually present in low-cost producers like Costco Wholesale

because they make a profit despite charging less for the services and goods they provide.

- When we talk about business reputation, an invincible amount of advantage comes with intangible things like intellectual property and brand awareness.

- **Repeat Purchase Business Model** – For any business, bringing in new customers is always a very expensive and difficult process. On the other hand, it is much easier and simple when the business is selling its products and services to customers who already exist within their chain. New customers definitely bring more growth, but that is not an easy task to achieve. That is why companies who are at the top of the list in terms of growth stocks usually introduce the concept of subscribers so that in order to get a product or service continuously, they keep paying after regular intervals. The products such companies are selling are usually something that will exhaust faster, leading to increased demand.

- **Financial Resilience** – The financial market health is something growth companies do not have to worry about when they have sufficient internal cash flow to fund their own growth in the future. But don't get me wrong. I am not saying that the growth companies have to generate a lot of profits from their first day of operation. What these growth companies do is that they reinvest all their profits from the initial days into their own business so that the growth process can be accelerated. But this can also lead to certain losses over the short-term. If the company is incurring such losses on a regular basis, then they have to look for new capital from other investors.

- **Strong Appreciation of Past Price** – There is usually a trend in the high-growth companies that they show a consistent period of growth, and they keep on winning. When the company is performing well, the stock remains way above the market, and in such a case, the share price increases.

Merits and Demerits of Growth Investing

Let us first start by checking the merits of this form of investing –

- **Rapid Growth** – Just like this term suggests, when you are into growth investing, you are investing your money in a company that is already in a period of high growth, and as far as the future is concerned, the stocks of the company are expected to continue growing. This means that the stock price is going to be increasing sustainably. This is something similar to what happened in the internet sector back in the 1990s.
- **Transcend the Trend** – You can call a company to be in a dynamic business when you notice

that they are showing sustained growth of 10-12%, and this growth rate is present even when the overall market is going through a slump or is stagnant. This means that if the growth stock is strong, it will have the ability to transcend the trend.

- **Long-Term Dominance –** If you look at the blue-chip value stocks like those of General Electric, Microsoft, or Walmart, you will realize that they were not always where they are today. They were growth stock aspirators in the beginning, and then the investors started investing in them, which set them up as a strong company for many more years to come.

Now, let us see what the demerits of growth investing are –

- **High Level of Volatility –** Since these companies have a high amount of volatility, they can also stand to lose their money as quickly as they had initially gained it. So, if you are investing in these companies, you also have to realize that your tolerance for risk has to be high and that market sentiment can lead to a decrease in the price of stock suddenly.

- **Long Term –** You have to keep in mind that growth investing is more of a long-term strategy, and you are not going to achieve anything in the short-term. So, if you are more into day trading or realizing immediate profits, growth stocks are not for you.

- **Vast Research –** Before investing in growth stocks, there is a substantial amount of research involved. The entire concept of growth investing is based on the fact that you have to pick a company that is poised for growth. But this is not such an easy task, and you have to understand a lot of indicators before you can finally decide the company to settle for.

74

Value Investing

In this section, we are going to discuss the concept of value investing in which the investors have to select stocks that are being traded at a value that is less than its book value or intrinsic value. When these investors think that certain stocks are being underestimated by the market, they ferret out stocks.

How Does It Work?

The main idea behind value investing is pretty simple – you will be able to save quite an amount of money when you are aware of the actual value of something, and you buy it on sale. A similar concept is then applied to the stock market. The valuation of a company does not change even when the stock of the company is on sale, and it has lowered in price. Even if there have been huge fluctuations in the price of the stock, it doesn't mean that the value of that company has gone through fluctuations as well.

So, if you want to engage in value investing, you have to do some digging of your own and research about the companies so that you can find the stocks which have a higher value, and yet the stocks are trading at a discounted price. The investor can then buy those stocks and hold them for a long time, after which they will get handsome profits by selling them at an appropriate price.

If the shares of a particular company are being undervalued, that is when the stocks are discounted. The valuation of any stock can be found out with the help of several metrics. Different types of financial analyses are used to find out the intrinsic value, and this involves going through the financial performance of the company, its business model, brand, competitive advantage, and target market. I am going to explain some of the metrics in this section here –

- **P/B or Price-to-book** – This is also referred to as the book value, and with the help of this metric, you can judge the value of the assets held by a company with respect to its stock price. The stock will be considered to be undervalued if its price is less than the assets' value.

- **P/E or Price-to-earnings** – Through this, whether the stock price has been influenced by all the earnings or not can be found out.

- **Free Cash Flow** – This is basically the amount you get after you have subtracted the expenditures of a company from the revenue generated by the company's operations. Thus, when all the expenditures have been cleared, what remains is the free cash flow. So, if free cash flow is being generated by a company, then it means that they are also going to have some amount of money left that they can reinvest in the future of their company or choose to distribute among the shareholders.

These were only some of the basic metrics that are used, and in reality, there are way more than these three.

Principles of Value Investing

I am going to brief you on the three basic principles of value investing that you should know in order to get started.

- **Don't Skip On Research** – If you want to profit from value investing, your research has to be thorough, and you have to know everything about a company before you actually invest your money in it. Your focus should be on those companies that have been paying regular dividends to its shareholders for years. So, whether the company is actually making it big on media or not is not really a big concern in the case of value investing.

78

- **Always Diversify** — Value investing is all about diversifying your assets, and your portfolio should comprise different types of investments and not just one. This will prevent you from incurring any serious loss.

- **Be On The Lookout For Steady Returns** — Everyone in the stock market thinks that they have come here to make money fast, but with value investing, that approach is not going to help you. Your focus should be on companies that can give you steady returns over the long-term and not extraordinary returns once in a while.

Merits and Demerits of Value Investing

Let us first discuss the merits of this approach of investing.

- **Substantial Returns** — This is definitely the main advantage of engaging in value investing. The returns that you are going to get with it are more than average in the long-term. This is because, in the beginning, the stocks that are purchased are underpriced, but when they are sold, they have gone above their intrinsic value.

- **Power of Compounding** – If you have been in the stock market, you are already aware of the power of compounding – how your money expands more in the long-term and value investing is all about that. In the course of time, there will be a dramatic increase in the interest you are getting, and you will be gaining from the interest that you received on interest.

- **Lesser Volatility and Risk** – You are not exposing yourself to too much risk if you engage in value investing because the volatility is less than several other strategies. You do not have to worry about the price fluctuations happening daily because you are not going to buy today and sell tomorrow. You are able to minimize the timing mistakes because of the buy and hold strategy followed in value investing.

Now, here are some of the demerits that you should be aware of –

- **Long-Term Approach** – One of the major demerits of the process of value investing is that even though you stand to get huge returns, but that is in the long-term and not now. So, once you have invested your money, it will have to stay locked up for a considerable period of time.
- **Difficulty to Identify Companies** – This is another drawback because the entire concept of value investing is based on the fact that you have to identify the companies that are undervalued, and this is not an easy task at all. You will have to possess a certain level of expertise in order to identify the value

companies correctly. Yes, you can work hard and go through all the fundamentals, but there will always be certain things that will be out of your control, and so there is no surety as to whether you will make the right decision or not.

- **Patience** – You can benefit from this form of investing only if you can maintain your level of patience. You have to understand that value investing is not everyone's cup of tea. If you are someone who prefers reaping benefits in the short-term, then you will find it difficult to hold your patience over the long-term. Moreover, at times, value investing in a company might also mean that you have to hold your position, not for months but years, and wait for the time when the market sentiment takes a turn in your favor.

Chapter 5: Forecasting the Trends in Stock Market

If you want to make profits in the stock market, you have to brush up on your skills of forecasting the trends of the stock market because that will help you determine in which way the market is going to move. Predictions are made after considering a lot of factors and not one, and in this chapter, I am going to explain the process of forecasting the market with respect to different methods of analysis.

Fundamental Analysis

Before we move on to the depths of fundamental analysis, you have to understand what it means. In simpler terms, fundamental analysis is a process that will help you to analyze the intrinsic value of security after the examination of different financial and economic factors. All the factors that can leave an impact on the value of the security are studied through fundamental analysis, and this includes both micro and macroeconomic factors. The main goal of this process is to help you understand whether a particular security is overvalued or undervalued with respect to its current price. Things like the strength of any particular industry or the overall state of the economy are taken into consideration for this analysis.

Types of Fundamental Analysis

Since fundamental analysis involves a vast range of concepts from the quality of management of a company to its revenue, the different fundamental factors are divided into two categories which we are going to discuss in this section —

Quantitative Analysis

The first category is quantitative analysis, which involves numerical terms or anything that can be quantified. In simpler terms, this form of analysis takes into consideration those factors of a business that can be measured – which means financial statements. The most important things in a financial statement that are utilized in the fundamental analysis are cash flow statements, balance sheets, and income statements. This will give you the idea of the resources that are controlled or owned by a business at any point in time and a company's equity, liability, and assets. You will also get an idea of the overall performance of the company from the revenues that it is bringing in.

Qualitative Analysis

The core aspects of fundamental analysis are mostly qualitative rather than quantitative, and the major factors that are analyzed are as follows –

- One of the first factors is the business model of a company. You have to find out what it is that the company does, and if you think that it is a pretty simple task, then trust me; it is not that easy as it seems.

- The next thing that falls under this category is competitive advantage. This is a factor that determines whether a company is going to be successful in the long-term or not. If competitive advantage has been achieved by any company, the shareholders also profit well over the course of time.

- Then comes management – which is considered to be one of the core concepts that you should look into if you want to invest in a company. One of the ways in which you can do it is by looking up the corporate website of the company and checking the qualifications and

resumes of the people at the topmost
positions.

- Lastly, corporate governance is the next most
  important thing in fundamental analysis
  because it analyzes what policies the company
  has launched and responsible the management
  is. Everyone wants to be in business with a
  company that is not only transparent and fair
  but also ethical.

Importance of Fundamental Analysis

Here are some of the ways in which fundamental
analysis is going to be helpful –

- Since this form of analysis scans the market,
  the economy, and the industries, it helps in
  predicting what the future price of any security
  will be. Certain parameters are used by the
  analysts to predict the future stock price.
- The valuation of a company is also determined
  by this analysis. You will come to know whether

87

a company is overvalued or undervalued. Once you know this, making decisions will become easier. If the intrinsic value is more than the current market price of the security, then the investor should buy the stock. On the other hand, if the intrinsic value is less than the current market price of the security, then the investor should sell the stock. Thus, stock picking becomes easier with fundamental analysis.

- The next benefit of fundamental analysis is that it helps you in evaluating whether the management of the company is good and responsible or not.

- You will also be able to judge whether the company has the ability to beat its competitors over a period of time so that you can find out once you invest your money, whether you can be in a strong position in the future or not.

- Lastly, you can also determine the financial strength of a company with the help of fundamental analysis and whether the company will be able to repay its debts. The financial performance of any company is definitely the ultimate thing that everyone looks forward to, no matter how good the management is.

If you are into long-term investments, you should not skip on fundamental analysis at all because it will help you to determine whether the company is suitable for a long-term investment.

Technical Analysis

Now, we are going to discuss the second form of analysis, which is also known as technical analysis, and it is mainly based on market data from historical records and also on behavioral economics. Among all forms of technical analysis, the two most common forms are technical indicators and chart patterns. In simpler words, we can say that technical analysis is nothing but a blanket term, and all the different types of strategies that are present under it will help you understand price action. One of the common things among all forms of technical analysis is that they will help you understand whether the ongoing trend in the market is going to continue in the future as well or not. Also, if the prediction is that the trend is not going to continue, then the technical analysis will help you to understand whether the trend is going to reverse.

Similarly, the chart formation is one of the aspects of technical analysis that helps sellers to understand which would be the best point for entry or exit into the trade. For example, the likeliness of a breakdown can be determined by analyzing the moving averages over different periods of time.

What Are Price Patterns?

Price patterns are usually used in technical analysis to determine the phase of transition between falling and rising trends. A set of curves or trendlines are used for identifying these price patterns. A reverse pattern is usually achieved when a specific price pattern signifies the trend direction to change. Similarly, a continuation pattern is when the existing direction is followed by a trend in the same way after a short pause. Both future price predictions and current price movements can be predicted with price patterns.

Trendlines

If you want to be able to forecast the price in the market, then understanding trendlines is something you should engage in. With the help of these lines, it will be easier for you to identify which are the areas of resistance and support in a price chart. These lines are basically straight lines with the help of which you can connect different ascending troughs and descending peaks in a particular chart.

Continuation Patterns

Like I already told you before, a continuation pattern is basically a price pattern that will show the continuation of the existing trend but after a temporary interruption. It can happen when amidst the downtrend, the bears relax for a while or when amidst the uptrend, the bulls take a short pause.

What Are Technical Indicators?

Just like price patterns, technical indicators are used in the forecast of price movements in the market, and in order to do this, they use different types of perspectives. In any particular time frame, the strength and direction of price movement are determined by technical indicators.

Some of the uses of technical indicators are as follows –

- The first and foremost function of these indicators is to alert you, and in some cases, they are even used as an alerting system for letting the traders know when there will be a breakout of support. To signify the breakout of resistance, a positive divergence act is used.
- Technical indicators are also used to confirm certain patterns or other technical tools like several candlestick patterns.
- You can use the technical indicators for predicting the movement of prices in the future.

But in order to reap the benefits of these technical indicators, here are certain things that you should keep in mind –

- You should not perform any investments or trades by depending solely on indicators.

- Implement other technical tools along with the technical indicators. For example, if you use the technical indicators to identify the different entry and exit points, then you should also use trendlines and candlestick chart patterns to confirm those points.

- You should keep your focus on 2-3 technical indicators at a time and not more than that; otherwise, you are just going to end up confusing yourself.

Volatility Theory

Volatility in itself signifies how much rise or fall the price of the stock of a particular company has to go through over a certain period of time. When the volatility of stocks is high, they undergo a way larger amount of dips and spikes in the price, whereas when the volatility of stocks is low, they undergo a more or less consistent pattern of loss or gain. Both the stock price and other variables are considered in order to calculate the volatility in a market.

How Are Market Prices Affected By Volatility?

In the case of stocks, when there is an increase in volatility, there is a decline in the price of stocks. Similarly, when there is a decrease in volatility, there is an increase in the price of stocks. But do you know why stocks decline with an increase in volatility? It is mainly because a business is considered to be deteriorating when there is a decline in the price of stocks, and this means that it is of high risk to investors to invest their money in such a business that is already in tatters. And thus, the price keeps fluctuating on a daily basis, which indicates greater volatility.

On the contrary, when there is an increase in the prices of stocks, it can be concluded that the business is going through a good phase and is currently in a stable state.

So, the price fluctuations on a daily basis are also small, which indicates a lower level of volatility.

Volatility and Investors

Even if you look at the historical records, you will understand that there is a clear relationship between volatility and the performance of stocks in the market. In fact, it has been noticed that there is a greater chance for the market to go on a downward spiral if there is high volatility. And there is a higher chance of a market to go in the upward direction if there is lower volatility. So, keeping your expected returns in mind, you, as an investor, can align your portfolio in a way that will be in proper alignment with the volatility.

There are several factors that have the ability to affect the volatility of a market, and this includes both national and regional economic factors. Things like change in interest rate policies and tax rules can lead the market in a different direction, and this has a direct effect on the volatility as well. Some other things that can affect volatility are special aspects belonging to any particular industry or inflation trends. For example, the prices of stock of oil companies will take a hit and be triggered to increase if there has been some massive weather event in areas that produce oil.

How to Anticipate the Market?

If you want to know what the future state of the market is going to be or where it is headed, you can take the help of leading indicators. So, if you have received the correct signal, you will have the upper hand, and you can ride the entire end by entering the market at the right time. But you also have to keep in mind that leading indicators might not be 100% correct at all times, and that is why they are never used alone and are used in combination with other forms of technical analysis. In this section, I am going to explain some of the major leading indicators and how they can help you anticipate the market. One of the reasons why different indicators sometimes show different signals is that they do not follow the same calculations.

Relative Strength Index or RSI

This is truly one of the most popular technical indicators, and it falls under the oscillatory category. The primary function of the RSI is to help traders and investors figure out the momentum of the market and identify whether the securities are in an oversold or overbought condition. Some other things that you can find out with the RSI are hidden divergence signals and the state of divergence. When you receive a signal with the help of the RSI, it is concluded that the market is going to reverse, and thus, it is a signal for the trader that they should either exit or enter a position.

The value of RSI ranges from 0 to 100. A market is said to be in an overbought condition if the value of RSI is more than 70. On the other hand, a market is said to be in an oversold condition if the value of RSI falls below 30. But like I already mentioned before, one of the drawbacks of following leading indicators is that you might get a false or premature signal every now and then and so it might happen that there is no reversal in the market and it continues to be in its current state for an extended period of time.

Stochastic Oscillator

Just like the RSI, the stochastic oscillator is also one of the most important leading indicators that will help you decide the state of the market and its future trend. The main purpose of this indicator is that it helps in performing a comparison between the previous trading range and the recent closing prices.

The main idea working behind this indicator is that the momentum of the market changes much more instantly than price or volume and so you can predict the direction in which the market is going to move. If the reading provided by the stochastic oscillator is more than 80, then you can conclude that the market is in an overbought state. Similarly, you can come to

99

the conclusion that the market is oversold if the value of the stochastic oscillator dips below 20.

But you might get false signals from the stochastic oscillator as well, especially if the market is currently too volatile. Any false signal has the power of affecting your trades, but you can prevent that by using several other technical indicators along with the stochastic indicator.

Williams %R

This is the Williams percent range and has a lot of similarities with the stochastic oscillator. But the major difference between the both is that the Williams %R is for a negative range on the scale and so its values are between 0 and -100, where the overbought signal is given by -20, and oversold signals are given by -80. But this indicator has a very responsive nature, which means that even when the current price does not follow the trend, the indicator will move will small highs and lows. So, you might be getting some

100

premature signals. This is also the reason why -10 and -90 are usually preferred by certain traders for extreme price signals.

OBV or On-Balance Volume

This is also a momentum-based leading indicator that you should know about if you want to forecast the trends in the market. In order to predict the market price, this particular indicator takes volume into consideration. Any changes in volume are noted down whenever the price does not change by an equivalent amount. Usually, such a situation indicated that there would be an imminent increase or decrease in price. But if there has been a huge volume announcement that is bound to take the market up by surprise, then you might get false signals from the OBV.

Chapter 5: Forecasting the Trends in Stock Market

Chapter 6: Day Trading

Initially, active trading was not open to everyone, and so only those who belonged to major trading houses, brokerages, or other large financial institutions were the ones who were able to engage in active trading. But now, with trading houses becoming online and the rise of the internet, it is possible for every investor to try their hands at active trading, and in this chapter, we are going to discuss one of the most lucrative forms of active trading – day trading.

What Is Day Trading?

The main aim behind day trading is short-term profit, and investors buy and sell stocks on the same day. They do not aim for huge profits but small profits on every trade. These small profits then compound over a period of time and make a huge chunk of money. But if you want to perform day trading successfully, you cannot do it between jobs or businesses and treat it as your main job.

Day trading takes full advantage of the concept of volatility. In fact, it is the market fluctuations that will fetch you profits in this case. Day traders find stocks that have the tendency to bounce about all throughout the day, no matter what the reason is. It can be because of a bad or good earnings report, market sentiment, or some good or bad news. Another thing to note is that day traders mostly rely on liquid stocks because this gives them the freedom to move into a position and move out of it very quickly irrespective of the stock price.

But you have to remember that day trading is not everyone's cup of tea because it requires you to stay committed to a great extent, and there is also a huge amount of risk involved. Moreover, timing is a big factor as to how the trade is going to play out, and you need to take care of that too. Also, if you want to efficiently capitalize on every potential intraday price movement, then you have to possess a sufficient amount of capital as well.

Which Traders Use This Strategy?

Day trading should by pursued by traders who have already got a taste of what trading is because, in day trading, you have to make a whole lot of decisions in a very short time span. There are tons of psychological biases that can end up pushing you to make the wrong decisions, and you definitely don't want that to happen to you; otherwise, you will lose a lot of money. There will always be a shot of adrenalin in your blood when you are trading, but you have to learn how you can keep your emotions away from the trade, and only then can you succeed.

So, before you dive into it full time, I would advise you to try day trading with a demo account – see if it is working out for you and if it is, then you can try it for real. These practice exercises will prepare you for the real world. Also, you should be willing to commit your day to trade if you want to proceed with this.

What Are the Advantages of Day Trading?

In this section, I am going to walk you through some of the major advantages of day trading –

- **Easy To Start** – I have to mention this at first because compared to several other types of trading, day trading is pretty easy to start. All you need is a stable internet connection and a laptop, the initial requirements have already been fulfilled, and then you can work your way up from there. But this easy nature of day trading also acts as a double-edged sword because there are so many traders who lose money just because they dive into day trading without proper knowledge, thinking that they can simply wing it. But it is not like that, and you have to educate yourself about how it works and what strategies you can use, and only then you can make sufficient profits.

- **Make Money Quickly** – Day trading can help you make some serious amount of money and quite quickly. You simply have to figure out a profitable strategy and carry it out consistently with discipline.

- **Overnight Risk Not Present** – When you hold your position overnight, there are a lot of risks associated with it because if there is a sudden announcement and the market sentiment changes, you might find yourself making huge losses in the morning. But with day trading, there are no such chances because you are not holding the position overnight. You are buying and selling assets on the same trading day.

How to Effectively Use This Strategy to Make Profits?

If you want to be successful in your day trading endeavor, then here are some things that you should follow –

- **Gain Knowledge** – When it comes to day trading, the statement "Knowledge is power" holds more meaning than anything else because knowledge is everything here. Every event and every piece of news can cause market fluctuations, and you have to capitalize on those fluctuations. But first, you have to know when those fluctuations are going to happen, and for that, you have to stay up-to-date. Homework is very important, and you should not skip it. Start by making a list of

108

stocks you are interested in because you cannot possibly keep researching about an endless number of stocks.

- **Start Small** – Most traders who fail make the mistake of diving into day trading with everything they have, and this is exactly the kind of behavior that is going to give you losses. When you are just starting out, choose a couple of stocks and stick to them. When you have just a few stocks in hand, the whole process of spotting and tracking opportunities becomes way easier.

- **Select Liquid Shares** – These are shares that are high in volume, and you have to keep in mind that day trading is about ending your trade before the day ends. So, your shares have to be liquid so that you can be quick.

- **Always Have A Stop Loss** – If you want to make good profits, having a stop loss is crucial. This is basically a price that you set from before, and you will not cross this price. The main aim of having a stop loss is to prevent your emotions from getting the better of you. If you are into short selling, then stop loss becomes all the more important to you.

- **Book Profits Timely** – There are so many traders who give in to greed and are thus, not able to book their profits at the right time. So, what you should do is look for multiple trades and keep booking small profits consistently.

- **Choose Your Entry And Exit Carefully** – The place where you enter a trade and exit from it determines your revenue, and so these two points should be determined after careful research. It is usually during the first half an hour of a trade that fluctuation in prices is at their highest level.

- **Find The Breakout Point** – You should keep an eye on the charts from time to time so that you can find the breakout point. This will help you find out where the resistance and support levels are with respect to the stock price.

- **Don't Go Against The Market –** One of the biggest mistakes that traders can make in day trading is going opposite to the trend. If the market is already in a bull phase, then your expectation should be that the stock is going to rise, and you should take your position accordingly. But if you take a short position, you might incur losses. So, for day trading, understanding the course of the market is very crucial.

- **Don't Over-trade –** Lastly, I would advise you not to over trade because that is one of the most common mistakes traders make. You should select a few stocks and stick to them. Emotional biases can lead you to believe that you need to trade more, but trading more can also mean losing whatever you have gained on that day. So, knowing your limits is very important, and you cannot break those limits.

An Example of Day Trading

Let us say that your stop loss is at $0.04, and your target is $0.06. You have a total of $30,000 in your trading account. The maximum risk that you are willing to take for every trade is $300. Keeping your stop loss in mind, for each trade, you can take a total of 7,500 shares ($300/0$0.04) and still remain within your limit of $300 per trade.

This strategy can play out in multiple ways, and I am listing them here for you –

- Total number of profitable trades is 60 which means 60 x 7,500 shares x $0.06 = $27,000
- Total number of losing trades is 45 which means 45 x 7,500 shares x $0.04 = $13,500

- Net profit from the day = $13,500 ($27000 - $13,500)

This is only a theoretical example, and in order to find out the actual net profit, you also have to subtract the commissions that you had to pay on the trade.

What Is the Risk/Reward in This Strategy?

The risk/reward ratio will basically tell you how much profit you can make on any particular trade as compared to the amount you are willing to lose. Now, as you already know, in the case of day trading, traders move in and out of the market in a short span of time, and so they make the best use of trading signals and short-term patterns. That is why every trade also has its own stop loss. The number of cents, ticks, or pips that a trader is willing to put at risk for a trade is determined by the stop loss.

Let us say that you are willing to risk an amount of $0.10 for buying the stock of Company X at $10, and so, you place a stop loss at $9.90. So, if we assume that there will be no slippage, then your risk will be limited to $0.10, and the potential profit that you are going to get at the end of the trade is going to compensate you for the risk that you are taking.

Now, let us say you have performed your research, and you think that the price of a stock is going to go up to $10.20, then the profit that you will get is $0.20. If we compare your potential reward and potential risk, then you will see that the former is twice that of the latter. The risk/reward ratio, in this case, will be equal to 0.5 ($0.10 / $0.20). So, if we are to say in simpler words, you are taking a risk that is half the equivalent gain. The lower the ratio of risk/reward, the better it is for you, especially when you are trading because this will limit your losses. No matter how high your risk tolerance is, if you want to minimize losses and maximize your profit, then your risk/reward ratio should be low.

When you are into day trading, you have to bring a balance between your risk/reward ratio and your win rate. If your risk/reward ratio is too high, then even a high win rate cannot help you in any way. Similarly, if your risk/reward ratio is good, but your win rate is low, it would not be profitable for you.

The chances of your risk/reward ratio to be high are more when your win rate is more. But let us say that your risk/reward ratio is 1.0 and your win rate is 60%, then you can be profitable, but the situation will be better if the risk/reward is below 1.0 and win rate at 60%.

But if you have a win rate of 40%, then you can make a profit if your risk/reward is less than 0.6, and this should not include the commissions.

In the ideal situation, if we assume that your win rate is 50% or less than that, then you should keep your ratio of risk/reward at less than 0.65. If the ratio of risk/reward increases, the chances are that your win rate will decrease. Moreover, if you lose more, you have to win more in order to make up for those losses.

Chapter 7: Swing Trading

There are different techniques in which you can trade stocks and fulfill the financial goals that you had set for yourself, irrespective of whether they are long-term or short-term. And one such technique is swing trading, which we are going to discuss in this chapter.

What Is Swing Trading?

Swing trading is a special type of trading strategy that spans over a few days or even a few weeks, and you collect the gains from the securities in that period of time. In short, in swing trading, the trader will hold on to his trading position for more than one trading session, be it a long position or a short one. The ultimate goal of swing trading is that the trader wants to make the most out of a potential move in price. For this reason, there are some swing traders who particularly prefer trading in stocks that are highly volatile and are thus prone to much more movement. But there are also certain other swing traders who prefer using sedate stocks.

Among all other types of active trading, swing trading is really popular, and traders use technical analysis to find trades that have the potential to bring profits. One of the most important things to keep in mind with swing trading is that you have to do everything possible to decrease the downside risk and this means that even if you are following a price range that is relatively large, you have to place considerably thought in calculating position sizing.

Which Traders Use This Strategy?

In the previous chapter, you have already learned about day trading, which requires you to sit in front of the computer every day, and it is more like a full-time job rather than a part-time hobby. But if you are looking for a form of trading that will help you take the benefit of price movements in the market and yet does not require you to be as committed as day trading, then swing trading is the perfect strategy for you. In the case of swing trading, you are allowed to hold your position overnight.

What Are the Advantages of Swing Trading?

A swing trader is mainly focused on identifying a rising stock, and when the stock is increasing in value, the traders ride the wave, and then they have to figure out the best time to come out of the market so that they get to keep all the profits that they have made in the trade. In this section, I am going to walk you through some of the major advantages of this form of trading –

- **Narrow Focus** – The first and foremost benefit of swing trading is that your focus will lay upon short term trends that have the tendency to increase their value fast. The time frames that are present in swing trading are fixed in such a manner that identification of the trend momentum does not really take up much time and focuses entirely on core market movement. In order to make a trade, you definitely have to look through certain information, but they are not much widely dispersed. All you have to do is focus on certain key areas because swing trading is all about trends and prices.

- **Quick Results –** Now, although swing trading is not done on a daily basis but even then, each trade spans over either a few days or a few weeks, and so, you don't have to wait too long to know whether your strategy has been successful or not. This also makes it possible for the traders to tweak their strategies according to their requirements so that the strategy keeps bringing them profits in a consistent manner.

- **Possibility Of Monthly Income Generation –** Contrary to long-term investments, you do not have to wait for years for your returns in the case of swing trading, which makes it an excellent way of obtaining monthly income. Since everything happens in the short-term, you will have a clear idea of how much money you have put into the trades and how much money you have available with you. Your earnings can be maximized by doing somewhere around 5-6 trades in a week, each of which will span over 10 to 12 days.

- **Time-Saving –** Another major benefit of swing trading is that the trader does not have to give it too much time. If you are an investor who cannot stay put in front of the computer screen all day long, then swing trading might be what you are looking for as it can be done even when you are pursuing some other full-time job at the same time. All you need to do is become proficient in technical analysis, and things will be done even faster.

- **Efficient Risk Management** – Every type of trading has its own risks, and so does swing trading, but one of the best things about it is that the risk can be minimized efficiently as well. There is the concept of stop losses, and moreover, you are only making a handful of trades in a week, so you do not have to keep checking on too many investments at the same time.

How to Effectively Use This Strategy to Generate Profits?

Profit-making opportunities for swing trading exist not only in bull markets but in bear markets as well, and I am going to explain them one by one.

Here are some bull strategies that you should keep in mind –

- **Play The Uptrend** – When stocks are trending, they do not move in a straight line. Instead, they move in a pattern that is very similar to that of stairs, and this is called the uptrend. For the initial few days, the stock keeps going up, but then, after a few days, you might notice that it is going down. The major part of the trend which swing traders look for is when the stock is going upward, and after this comes the pullback. This is also known as the counter-trend, but once this phase is over, the upward movement of stocks continues again.

- **Make Most Out Of The Upside** – There is no certainty as to how long the counter-trend or pullback is going to last, and so, you should initiate your trade only when you notice that the stock is again on the rise. That is why figuring out the right entry point is so crucial. If you are not sure how a good entry point looks like, then here is an example – the stock should be trading at a level that is above the high of the previous day's pullback. Your stop out point will be the pull back's lowest point. This will be the point that will limit your losses because if the trade goes below this point, you will sell your position.

- **Enter The Trade Right** – A major part of making profits in a swing trade depends on your entry, so you need to work on perfecting it.

Now, let us move on to some important strategies to make profits in a bear market –

- **Make Most Out Of The Downside** – In the bear market, you have to make the best use of the downtrend. But even here, you cannot predict how long the downtrend is going to last, and so

it is advisable that you enter the trade only
when the stock has started showing
improvements.

- **Know When To Enter** – You can submit a swing
  trade with the help of a sell-stop limit order, or
  you can also purchase an option that is in-the-
  money.

An Example of Swing Trading

There are various ways in which you can make the best
out of the market swings and capitalize on them. In
this section, I am going to provide you with an example
to make the concept of swing trading even clearer.

You have to start by figuring out an ETF or a stock
which is trending in that week, and the bottoms are
sharp. Then, analyze the initial point of the trend and
see how the stock had performed then. Let us say the
stock has returned to the moving average thrice, and at
1.5% of the price, the stock has penetrated the moving

average. You should place a purchase order, and you should place it at 1% of the price of the instrument below the moving average.

The next thing that you should do once you have entered into the trade is that you should place a protective stop, and this should be reasonably in close proximity to your point of entry. You have to make it your mantra that you will take the profits that are near the upper channel line, but if you think that the market is strong enough, you can wait until the channel line is hit. But if you think that the market is not strong, then you have to grab the first opportunity at a profit you get.

What Is the Risk/Reward in This Strategy?

One of the major reasons why swing trading is so popular among people is that it takes full advantage of the price swings, and it either fades a rally or reversed back to the median position. As you already know that the first step is to filter out the stocks that are best for you, and then you have to be on the lookout for the correction or the short pause. The capitalization of a trend begins when the stock moves forward after the short pause. That is why swing trading offers the best use of capital and also one of the best risk/reward ratio to the traders.

This point, where the stocks take a pause, can be identified through various methods. You can check the past highs and lows and find out the support and resistance levels. The point where the stock had corrected is referred to as the swing high. There are others who are in the habit of using moving averages in order to find out the point of reversal from where they expect the stock to move back. Another way to determine is by using stochastics and determining whether the market is in an oversold or overbought condition, and this will help you figure out your entry point.

No matter which of these ways you ultimately choose, your main aim should be to choose an entry point that is perfectly aligned with the trend at a point that has the lowest amount of risk. The usual ratio of risk/reward that is followed by swing traders is 1:3 or more. The exit in the case of swing trading can either be made in one go or in two parts. Some traders follow a strategy where they exit partially at the previous swing low in a downtrend or a previous swing high in an uptrend. After that, they use their remaining position to ride the trend until they see that the momentum is coming to a halt.

There are other traders who have a fixed number of days during which they trade, say 10-12 days because they have already performed their research and backtesting has shown them how stocks are moving in a certain direction for that span of time no matter what the price is.

As far as short-term trading is concerned, the risk/reward ratio that you are going to get in swing trading is truly one of the best. Moreover, swing trading is not as fast-paced as day trading, which makes it easier to grasp for complete beginners. Lastly, I would like to say that swing trading is definitely one of the best forms of trading not only from the monetary gain point of view but also from the skills that you will learn in the process.

Chapter 8: Passive Investing

In this chapter, we are going to discuss a special type of investment strategy, which is known as passive investing. You can broadly call it as a kind of strategy that follows buy-and-hold policy and is all about getting handsome returns in the long-term.

What Is a Passive Investing Strategy?

Two of the most basic disadvantages linked with frequent trading are limited performance and a lot of trading fees, but both of these things can be avoided if you move to passive investing where the main goal is to build wealth over an extended period of time. In here, you will have to choose a security and then buy it. You will hold it for a long period of time before selling

131

it. Market timing or fluctuations in price over the short term do not bother the passive investors. In this case, they follow the assumption that when they are holding on to a security over a period of time, the market is going to provide them with positive returns.

The managers of passive investment strategy are of the belief that no matter what they do, it will not be possible for them to outthink the market and so keeping in mind the performance of the market, they try to match it. The portfolios are constructed in such a way that they are well-diversified, and they can replicate the market performance, but the presence of portfolios makes the process easier. If this were to be done for individual stocks, the process would have become much difficult and would have also required an extensive amount of research. The entire process of passive investing became easier in the 1970s because, at that time, the index funds were introduced, and after that, staying in line with the market and achieving similar returns became painless.

Which Traders Use This Strategy?

If the trader is more interested in long-term investments and is looking forward to capital gains as a mode of making money, then the passive investing strategy is the option they should go for. In such a case, the investors or traders are asked to choose an index fund, buy it, and hold it for a certain period of time until the market is in their favor, and they can make profits by selling. Usually, when the fund is held over a period of years, the returns increase by many folds because of the compounding effect of the stock market.

In short, if you are a trader or an investor who does not have sufficient time in their day-to-day schedule to monitor trades every day and you are looking for an option through which you can generate money in the long run and at the same time carry on with your other activities, then passive investment strategy is meant just for you. With a passive investing strategy, you will not be losing sleep over minor fluctuations that keep happening on a day-to-day basis because if you think of the long-term, you are going to get decent returns.

What Are the Advantages of This Strategy?

A passive investing strategy is something that more and more investors are approaching in today's world through ETFs and index funds. So, let us have a look at some of the advantages of this strategy —

- **Reduced Expenses** – According to reports, on a yearly basis, passive investing will cost you only about 0.20 percent in terms of fees. On the other hand, if you have a look at active investing reports, it shows that for active investing, it is about 1.35 percent. So, if you want to access the stock market and make money, but you do not

134

want to incur a huge amount of fees, then passive investing can really be a great way to do so because there are almost no hefty commissions. The fees are minimal too, and so whatever money you are making in the long-term will largely remain in your own hands, and only a nominal amount will be charges as admin fee.

- **Diversification** – Start by checking the asset class you want to invest in and then select an index. Whether you should sell or buy anything will largely depend on the inherent strategy of the index that you have chosen. Let us say the S&P 500 Index – the inherent strategy of this index is that it will give you the ownership (about a fraction) of the top 500 companies in the United States.

- **Fewer Taxes** – You will not have to pay any huge amount of taxes with passive investing because the number of times you are buying or selling stocks is reduced, and so the taxes related to those investments is also reduced.

- **Simplicity** – The simplicity of investing in a passive strategy is also one of the reasons why it is suitable for beginners. You will always be aware of where your money is going and what is happening to it. Moreover, it will be much easier for you to remove and then reinvest.

But there are certain disadvantages that you should be aware of too, and so I am listing them here –

- **Stock Concentration** – One of the major disadvantages of being involved in passive investing is that in certain cases, they get so much concentrated on the large-cap funds that your money will also be going only into the top 50 or top 100 companies. So, you will not be able to take advantage of any other opportunity that arises in the stock market, which, in turn, leaves your money vulnerable to several regulatory and political events.

- **Limited Returns –** With a passive investment strategy, you can never expect your investments to beat the market because they will always remain in line with the market. And I am not saying this is a bad thing – you will be playing on the safer side, but at the same time, you will be depriving yourself of extraordinary returns.

How to Effectively Use This Strategy to Generate Profits?

Before going into the different ways in which you can engage in passive investing, you should know what this strategy calls for in general –

- You will first have to find a collection of holdings for the long-term, and they should not be from any one sector or industry. They should be spread over a number of industries, if possible even countries and market capitalization sizes.

- No matter how much distressing times are or you feel that the holdings are no longer what they appeared to be, you should not sell them because they will regain their value in the long term.

- Engaging in passive investing does not mean that you will leave your account as it is once you have invested. You have to keep investing by depositing fresh cash from time to time into your account with the brokerage, and then you should reinvest your dividends.

- Another thing to keep in mind is that you should try your best to keep the costs as low as you can.

Historical evidence about passive investing suggests that no matter what the circumstances are, a passive investing strategy will work well in most of them. So, even if the investors seem to find themselves in situations where they are irrational, passive investing will protect them from anything bad happening to their money. Moreover, with passive investing, you do not have to spend hours behind understanding finance and accounts, and you do not really have to commit too much of your time behind it.

The best forms of passive investments strategies have been explained below –

- **Real Estate** – It is true that in recent years, the real estate industry has undergone various types of fluctuations, but even then, when people are seeking long-term returns, it is real estate they turn to. This is even more valid in the case of rental properties, which can give the owner a regular source of income once furnished well. In order to get a rental property,

you only need a 20% down payment, and then
you can get money coming in every month
once you get reliable tenants for your property.

If you think you will not have the time or energy
to manage rental property all on your own, then
you can try and research more about REITs or
Real Estate Investment Trusts. These are known
to pay dividends to investors from 90% of their
total taxable income.

But if you are looking more like a middle-
ground solution, then real estate crowdfunding
can be good for you. You can choose whether
you want to be in debt investments or income
investments, and this is applicable to both
residential and commercial properties.

- **Peer-to-Peer Lending** – This industry is also
termed as crowdfunding, and even though it

came about just about ten years ago, the industry has increased by huge amounts ever since then. In this strategy, you will be lending money directly either to a business entity or a person, and there are several platforms through which you will remain connected as borrowers or lenders. The returns in this type of strategy are usually between 7-12%.

- **Dividend Stocks –** When it comes to generating passive income, dividend stocks are the best way to do so. When profits are incurred by the different public companies, the investors get dividends, which are nothing but a portion of the profits that this company has generated. Now it is up to the investors as to whether they want to reinvest the dividend or they want to keep it in their pockets. The number of dividends that you are going to get from a company will vary from year to year, and this amount is not the same for every company.

141

- **Index Funds** – Lastly, there are index funds, which are also a great way of engaging in passive investing. As you already know, the index funds are a special type of funds that are related to one particular market index. Their main aim is to replicate the performance of the index that they are based on, and they are managed passively. So, unless and until there is a shift in the index, there is no change in the underlying securities as well. And thus, the investors are in luck because they experience lower turnover rates and lower management costs, which means if you think from the point of view of tax, then index funds can be a great way of investing passively.

In short, any form of passive investment can actually simplify your life and help you generate income in the long-term.

An Example of Passive Investment Strategy

Both ETF and mutual funds are examples of passive investment strategies. One of the best examples of this strategy would be if an investor buys an index fund that follows one of the major indices like the Dow Jones or the S&P 500. If the constituents of these funds switch between themselves, the index funds will also undergo changes. When a company is leaving, the index fund will sell the stock, and when a company is being added, the index fund will buy the stock.

What Is the Risk/Reward in This Strategy?

For the management of the portfolio in passive investment, several dynamic approaches are now being adopted so that everything is in line with the goals you have set for that particular portfolio. The objectives of this strategy are largely driven by risk/reward profiles. The asset allocation that is done in the passive investment strategy is helpful in balancing the risk and reward. The weights of different assets that are present in the portfolio are judged, and then it is assessed whether the ultimate objective is met or not.

The strategy to follow is determined after you have selected the risk/reward ratio. You can measure the reward through appreciation over a period of time, whereas risk is usually depicted by the standard deviation. Thus, risk will show you the volatility of the stock.

Chapter 9: Bonus Secrets and Tips to Becoming a Top Trader

No matter what market you are trading in, if you want to be a profitable trader, there are certain tips and tricks that you should know about. At first glance, it might seem that booking huge profits is a very easy task whereas, in reality, it is not. If you look at the statistics, it says that over 80% of the newbie traders fail initially, and then they turn to hobbies that are safer and do not include any loss of money. You will not see these failure rates being published by the brokerage industry because they do not want to show these to you, as this will most likely scare off people who are looking forward to opening new trading accounts.

But don't worry; you can get success in your trading endeavor if you follow certain advice that I am going to give you in this chapter.

Have a Trading Plan

This is probably the most basic advice that you are going to get everyone in this field because this is the holy grail of trading. Whether you incur a profit or a loss from trade depends on the personal decisions you make, and those decisions will become so much easier when you have a well-outlined plan. And this is true not only for trading, but for any other endeavor in your life, the chances of you reaching the finish line with the trophy in hand become easier when you have figure out the path that you want to follow.

When you have a plan, you set your goals way in advance, and you also know what it is that you exactly want from the trade. There are several advantages to having a trading plan, but the major one out of all of them is that it gives you the chance to approach the trade with an objective mind and so in short, you will have greater confidence in you, and you can also keep your emotions at bay. When you are investing or trading, you will incur losses from time to time, but what you can't do is let your emotions get the better of you. Even if the loss that you incurred was emotionally draining, you have to get back up and plan for your next trade keeping your previous mistakes in mind.

Treat It Like Your Business

If you want to be successful in trading, you cannot simply take it lightly. If you think that it is just a hobby and you can get away with very little research and very little time devoted towards it, then you are wrong because no matter how small-scale your trading plan is, the research that you have to do to bring home profits is quite a lot. Even if you are not doing it full time, you can treat it as your part-time business and see it with equal importance.

If you have this firm belief in your mind that it is a hobby, then you cannot be fully committed to learning anything. If you think of it as a job, then you won't be able to enjoy the process, and all you will be bothered about is a big fat paycheck, which might not always be as you expected it to be. And when your expectations are not met, you think about quitting. So, you have to treat trading like a business, and like any other business, there will be ups and downs, and there will be stress, uncertainty, taxes, and risk. Don't worry if it is feeling intimidating at first because you can figure it out one day at a time. You have to learn the art of strategizing through sufficient research so that you can expand the potential of the trade.

Make the Best Use of Technology

As you already know that trading involves a lot of competition and in order to end the day with profits in your hand, you have to rise above the competition that comes in your way. You have to keep it in your mind that the person sitting in front of you has all the latest technology at his/her disposal, and they are utilizing it to their full potential. Analyzing markets and viewing all the details is very important for making the right decisions and charting platforms can help you do it the right way. If you want to avoid taking any wrong steps, then you can also try utilizing historical data in order to backtest your strategies.

With real-time updates from several platforms, you can keep yourself updated about the trades no matter where you are. You can be anywhere in the world and still engage in active trading. All you need is a high-speed internet connection and a smartphone, and you are all set to place the trades. Staying updated at all times is going to reward you in the best way by bringing you profits and also keep you up-to-date with any new products that are there in the market.

Keep a Check On Economic Calendars

I am going to tell you about a major trading secret that most people overlook, and that is keeping a check on the economic calendars. If you do this, you will be able to stay ahead of all the events that happen in the market and that have the ability to influence your trade. These events can move the market in a certain direction, and if you are able to use these events in the right way, then you can come up with a plan that will help you profit by anticipating and correctly predicting these events.

Some of the major influential events that will be broken down in these economic calendars are as follows –

- GDP announcements

- Decisions about interest rates

- CPI or Consumer Price index

- PMI or Purchasing Managers' Index

You will learn to be more organized and disciplined once you start keeping track of the economic calendars. And these are some of the qualities that you should inculcate in yourself as a trader. With technology becoming so advanced with each passing day, you do not have to keep track of the economic calendar on your own. You can leave the task on several apps and trading platforms, which will send you notifications whenever they find anything worthy of bringing into your notice. In fact, you can tweak the alert systems based on your requirement, and in order to do so, you do not have to give them any personal information whatsoever.

Have the Willingness to Learn

When you have the intention to learn, action will come on its own. So, the first step towards it involves having the intention and making a strong resolution to do something that will help you learn more about the stock market. But you can't just wing it and expect amazing results. You have to take it lightly and take it slow. You have to spend some time doing the thinking as to why you are approaching this endeavor in the first place and what are your hopes regarding the future. Ask yourself about the gains that you think you are going to have from this. You need to be prepared for the road ahead of you not only by reading up but also by mentally preparing yourself for it. All of this will help you slowly build your foundation in this respect, and slowly, you will also be able to set clear goals.

Once the part of decision-making is done, it is time that you decide to step your foot into the stock market and test something out on your own. It's true that you should not experiment or jump right into the process without any proper knowledge because the moment you do that, you are bound to end up losing a lot of money in the process. And when that happens, people usually quit trading altogether because of the discouragement. If you want to succeed, you have to give yourself a proper chance to do so, and that means you cannot quit just like that.

So, sign up for reputed newsletters, read authentic books, and do some research on the internet on the various ways in which you can know more about this market, and with time, you will be able to figure out what is appealing to you the most.

It is somewhat like going back to school. The only difference is that you are doing it to learn more about the stock market. You have to be obsessive about learning because the more you learn, the more it will benefit you. If you already have a full-time job, then you have to block time in your calendar for this research. You have to do it on a daily basis, no matter how much research you do. You have to stick to the schedule that you have made for yourself and learn to hold yourself accountable.

Give Considerable Thought Before Choosing Your Trading Style

As you know already, there are different types of stock trading, and before you settle for any one of them, you have to think carefully whether that type of trading would fit you or not. If you choose day trading, then you have to devote a fixed amount of time to trading on a daily basis. Then there is short-term trading in which you can hold your position for a period of few days, or you can also be a monthly or weekly trader depending on your time availability and devotion you want to show. But after you have chosen one form of trading, it does not mean that you cannot change your choice or shift to another form. The key to becoming successful is to first choose the style of trading that resonates with you.

You have to think from the perspective of your lifestyle because that is going to play a major role in the style of trading you choose. For example, if you are into day trading, it means that you have to spend the better part of the day in front of the computer and so it is definitely time-consuming. If you think you wouldn't be able to give much attention, then long-term trading of stocks is what you need. On the other hand, if you want to engage in short-term trading, then you have to inculcate a certain discipline in you and allow the stock to run for a certain duration of time so that you can exit at the right moment and bring home profits. Usually, trading becomes more intense when the time frame is short.

Choose the Right Broker

This is one of the most important steps because there are a lot of things in trading that can become limited if your broker is not providing you those features. If you don't want that to happen to you, then you have to make the right choice regarding a broker in the first place. But before you move on to the decision of a broker, choosing your trading style is important because that is what will determine the broker too.

Keep At It

If you want to be successful in trading, you cannot just give up after one loss. Remaining diligent is one of the things that are highly important for being successful in trading. Even if you have faced a little failure, keep reassessing your goals, and revisit them. Stay motivated and keep practicing good habits and leave the bad habits behind. This doesn't happen overnight, but patience will definitely pay you off in the long run. You cannot only stick to the trade when the times are good. You have to stick to it even when the times are bad and be truly passionate about what you are doing. If you want long-lasting success, this is the only way of achieving so.

Apart from what I have already mentioned above, I would like to say one last thing – if you want, you can also look for a mentor who will guide you. Seeking guidance from the right person will help in streamlining your learning process, and you will also be able to gain some valuable insight.

Chapter 9: Bonus Secrets and Tips to Becoming a Top Trader

Chapter 10: Common Mistakes Beginners Make and How to Avoid Them?

There can be a lot of factors because of which you have been making mistakes in the stock market, and impatience, exuberance, and ignorance are just some of them. But sometimes mistakes can be too grave and might cost you your entire capital, so you have to try your best to avoid these mistakes from happening. By the time you finish this chapter, you will be savvy about the common mistakes that happen with beginner investors, and you will also know how to maintain a cool composure while you are investing or trading.

Making Investments When You Are Not Ready

This is probably the most common mistake when it comes to the stock market. Most people think that since stocks are the most basic financial instruments – you can invest in the market whenever you feel like it – even when you are not ready. But this is not true. You not only have to be prepared for the investment financially, but you also have to prep yourself mentally before stepping in.

If you have any debts on you, especially the high-interest ones, you should not step into stock investing right now. First of all, use that extra cash to pay off your debt first, and then you can start investing in stocks. Let us say you are already paying a huge interest of 17% on your debts annually (and 17% is not an unusual rate), then whatever money you are investing in stocks will have to earn more than that so that you are at a good place financially. Now, as I told you before, according to reports, the average returns from the stock market are more or less 10% on an annual basis and not 17% or even near that. In fact, there have been several periods where it was lesser than 10%.

Another thing to keep in mind is that before you come into the world of stocks, I think it would be wise if you have your emergency fund set up first. Your aim should be to have at least twelve months' worth of living expenses stocked up so that even if there is a crisis, you are covered for a year during which you can look for some alternative job. Let us say you do not have an emergency fund, and your car needs a serious repair, or you have a huge medical bill to pay because of an emergency, what are you going to do in such cases? Your stocks will go out of your hand because you will be forced to sell them. Why fall in such a situation, when you can avoid it altogether by taking preventive measures?

Investing With No Market Knowledge

Let us say that you have a good financial standing and you do not have any debts and you have also set up your emergency fund, should you dive right in? Well, no, because you still haven't educated yourself about the workings of the stock market, and this is equally important for anyone who wants to make profits. 70% of the beginners enter the stock market because they have this dream of making a lot of money, but they seem to forget that the stock market is also the place where people lose millions just because they took an uninformed decision.

Imagine it in this way – you are in your first year of engineering degree, would you be able to design a hi-tech robot right away? No, right? Because you do not have the knowledge required to do so, but it will become easy for you once you know the technicalities. It is the same with the stock market. You cannot turn yourself rich overnight. You have to work hard and learn the strategies and then be patient about your investments or trades. Read more and more books and enroll for online courses from reputed websites, and if you are diligent enough, it will not take you much time to learn it all up. But don't start investing your money before you know the basics. You will end up losing your money.

Blindly Following Everyone Else

Trusting the wrong source and listening to any random person regarding what they think about a particular stock is the most common rookie mistake ever. Let us say that you are having a family gathering, or you have gone out with your friends, and you start having some financial discussion. The people around you start sharing their ideas on which stocks might be performing well and if there is any company that might be a big shot now. Or, you can even gather some random tips from the TV shows you watch. But does that mean you should follow those tips blindly? Absolutely not! For starters, you are not sure, or you do not have any idea about the expertise of the person stating those facts. And secondly, you cannot afford to lose your money on some random tip that you haven't researched yourself.

Beginners often think that following the trend in the market will keep them on the safe side. Well, if you think that way, then you are wrong because that is exactly what is going to land you in trouble. You have to have a full understanding of what is happening in the market if you want to make profits. Also, if anything sounds too good to be true, chances are that they are not, but it is always better to do your research.

Having Unrealistic Expectations

If you want to build a considerable amount of money by investing or trading on the stock market, then you have to realize something, that is, it is not something that will happen overnight or in a week. There is nothing called quick gains. You need patience and the right tactics to make it big. Unrealistic expectations can provoke you to make rash decisions. For example, you might end up putting money in a stock that you would actually need in the near future. You never know when the market turns in the opposite direction, and you end up losing all the capital that was indeed very important to you. Sometimes, once the market has taken a negative turn, it takes a few years for it to get back on track.

You have to expect volatility when you are investing in stocks. Like I told you before, the average return on an annual basis is 10% from stocks, but in some years, it can be 20% too, or in some other years, it can be 8%. If your goal is long-term, you will stand to make profits if you had chosen the right company, but if you have a short-term goal, there will be a lot of factors in play.

Paying High Commissions

Once you open an account with your online broker and you finally start investing or trading, you have to make sure you are not paying too much commission. Commissions are the fees that brokerages charge because of the orders you place. And this is something you should check before settling for any broker in the first place. The maximum commission that you should agree to pay is 2% of the total value of the trade. Let us say, you plan to place a trade that amounts to $1000, so according to the 2% rule, your commissions should amount to no more than 20$. If you do a bit of research, then you will find that there are lots of brokerages in today's world who charge as low as $7 or even less for every trade that you place. This ensures that even if you are placing considerably small trades, you are not going to cross that 2% margin.

2% of a trade that amounts to$350 makes $7. But let us say you want to place an even small trade like $100, then paying $7 as commissions would mean you are giving away 7%. So, if you want to achieve break-even, then you will have to make a profit of as much as 7%.

So, whether you are paying a high amount of commissions or not will totally depend on the amount of your trade and also the manner in which the broker decided to take its commission – does it have a fixed rate, or does the rate depend on the amount of trade?

Trading Too Much

If you think that you can trade as much as you want and that there is no limit, then you are wrong. Of course, there is no physical barrier, but when you are starting out, trading frequently will do you more harm than good. Moreover, if trading in the stock market is just a means for your secondary market, then it becomes even truer for you. You always have to keep your investment goals in mind before you start trading too much. When you trade frequently, you will end up overwhelming yourself.

As a beginner, you might be buying stocks from a few big and exciting companies, and then when you notice some more exciting companies, you might sell the stocks that you have in hand so that you can buy the others. You have to keep an eye on the trading fees that you are accumulating through this. Moreover, you might incur short-term capital-gains rates when you buy and sell stocks within the same year, and this rate is way more than the rate of the long-term.

Buying Penny Stocks

Before I explain to you why buying penny stocks is a mistake, let me explain what penny stocks are. These are basically stocks that are traded at a price where each share is in the range of $5, and some of them are even priced as low as $1. People get enticed to these shares because of one simple reason – they think they can buy a lot of shares of such companies even when they have only 100 dollars. But do you know where the problem lies? Well, these stocks are not reliable, and they sometimes even come from shady companies. Moreover, scammers manipulate them quite often, and they are also highly volatile.

The shares of such stocks are usually bought by scammers, and then they implement various strategies to hype up that stock. For example, they post about it on newsletters, online forums, and so on so that others get interested in the stock, and the price goes up. And when they achieve that, they go on and sell their shares. This results in a price plunge where the other investors who fell into the scam lose their money. Such schemes also have a special term, and that is – pump-and-dump scheme.

If you think that when you see a stock priced at as low as $1, you have struck a bargain, then you are wrong because it is highly likely that the stock will fall even more to as low as $0.10.

Trading Without Any Strategy

There are some traders, especially beginners, who think trading is like gambling. But NO! It's not. If you talk to any experienced trader, they will be able to tell you exactly what their investment goals are and what they have done to achieve those goals. They can also give you a clear figure of the amount of loss they can withstand at any particular point of time, and they also have their exit and entry points figured out. These are strategies and processes that you have to devise before you start trading. For an experienced trader, all of this comes naturally, and you have to work your way up to that point as well.

Beginners who are putting money in stocks, exit from any trade the moment they see that the prices have begun to fall and do you know what the worst thing is? There are some traders who think that a miracle is going to happen all of a sudden, and that will help them win a lot of money. There is no such thing as that. You win money, or you lose it based on the trading decisions you make. There are also times when you will notice traders getting stuck in one position simply because they think that trade is going to turn around, and they will get all their money back and what happens when it doesn't go the way they thought? They end up losing all the money. That is, you have to strategize your trades, and if you are looking for serious profits, you have to have a full grasp on what is happening in the market.

Letting Your Emotions Get the Better of You

I have already talked about trading psychology at length in Chapter 2, but I am going to tell you again –

don't let any of your emotional biases ruin the standing that you have created for yourself in the stock market. If you have been making successive losses and yet you choose to stay in the trade just because you 'feel' the price is going to rise, then you are doing it wrong. You are letting your emotions get the better of you, and you should not do that.

In the same way, if you decided to exit from a stock early, don't let that influence other trades for you. You have already exited the previous trade, and there is nothing you can do about it. So, why ruin the rest of the trades because of it? Your technical and fundamental research should not be compromised in any way whatsoever. Keep your ears open for any important announcement or news that is going to affect your stocks. When you are just starting out, all of this might seem overwhelming, but with time, it will become second nature to you too. You simply have to look past all your personal biases and make your trading decisions without letting your emotions come in the way.

Putting All Your Eggs In One Basket

I have talked about diversification at length throughout this book, and by now, you probably have a clear concept of it, but even then, there are plenty of traders who make this mistake knowingly. If you are investing your hard-earned money in only a few stocks, you are deliberately pushing yourself to get exposed to more risks than you cannot handle. Let's say that you have invested only in one stock, and your portfolio increases when that stock increases. But let us say that the price of the stock is reduced to 30%, then your entire capital will be reduced too. I cannot give you a fixed number as to the number of stocks that you should own, but I can definitely tell you this – you should have more than 15 stocks so that you are not exposing yourself to too much risk at a time.

But this doesn't mean that you should own 100 or even 50 stocks at a time because in that case, even if there is a major hike in the price of any one stock, your income would not be influenced much because by investing in too many stocks, you have reduced the amount invested in each stock. Also, when you have so many stocks in your portfolio, it will become even harder for you to keep a grasp on what is going on in the market. Anything between 10 and 20 would be a reasonable number of stocks to own.

Avoiding Rebalancing of Portfolio

Some people don't even notice that they are not balancing their portfolio in the right manner. Your first task is obviously to get the securities in the right proportion. For example, it can be something like 25% of your investments are in bonds 75% in stocks. Let us say, in a period of 5 years, the stocks have grown, and now they constitute about 90% of your portfolio. That is not the amount that you want to hold, but you overlook it. This increases your risk exposure even without you knowing it. That is when you are overdue for a portfolio rebalancing. In the example I gave above, you have to buy more bonds and sell a few stocks so that the proportion is adjusted to the decided percentage.

Waiting Too Long for an Unlikely Rebound

This is a very common mistake. Let us say that you had bought a few shares and you had predicted that their price will rise, but now, their price has fallen down. Suppose your initial investment was that of $2000, but the value of stocks has fallen down to make your invested capital amount to $1000. You will clearly lose all your faith and confidence in the company, but when you think about selling your shares, the only thought that will be looming over your mind is that if you sell the stocks, you will be losing as much as $1000.

There are investors who are quite stubborn, and they don't want to deal with that loss, so they decide to hang on and wait for a rebound to happen. They will wait so that at least the loss can be wiped out when they sell the stocks. But is this a smart move? I would say no. If you think that the company has lost its value, then the stock price is unlikely to go through any major increase in the near future.

What you should do is sell your shares so that you can at least take back that $1000 before facing any more loss. You can reinvest that amount in some other stock, which has the potential for growth, and it is more likely to grow in a more promising company than the one which has lost its value.

Now that you know about the common mistakes that people make in the world of the stock market, you will become aware of them and, hopefully, not make them yourself. Continue reading and enhancing your knowledge because that is the only way in which you can become more aware of what is going on in the market. Just like success stories, you should read about failures too because they will make you learn about strategies or habits that can lead to failures. You will also learn about new styles of management. Educate yourself on the various industries in the market so that you come to know about their challenges and also their prospects. There is no end to how much you can learn, but the more you learn, the fewer mistakes you will make.

Conclusion

Thank you for making it through to the end of *Stock Market Investing for Beginners*, let's hope it was informative and able to provide you with all of the tools you need to achieve your goals whatever they may be.

My goal in this book was to educate everyone about every aspect of the stock market and how you can make a living by investing and trading stocks. I am hoping that by now, you have a comprehensive idea of how the stock market works. If you have always been interested as to how the stock market works, but you were never sure about where to start, then this book right here can provide you all that you need to know as a beginner. I have given practical information and useful examples in every chapter to make the learning process easier for everyone.

As a beginner, you might lose some money trying your hand at different forms of trading and investments, but don't let those small losses define your path because no person has ever made it big in the market without incurring any loss in their life. What you have to do is learn from the mistakes that you are making so that they don't happen again. Make sure you have built your emergency fund, and you have set money aside for your day-to-day expenses before coming into the stock market. I hope the information provided in the book has helped you start a new chapter in your life, and I wish you all the very best on this journey. Remember that the stock market can help you fulfill all your dreams, and at the same time, mismanagement and bad judgment can lead you to lose all your money.

Finally, if you found this book useful in any way, a review on Amazon is always appreciated!

Glossary

Agent – An agent is a person or any securities firm that is responsible for representing the client whenever they are selling or buying any security. When the transaction takes place, the agent only performs the act of representation but does not own the security in any way.

Annual Report – An annual report is basically published by respective companies in which they show their operations and financial statements, and they issue this report to their shareholders. The publication of the annual report usually happens at the end of the fiscal year.

Assets – Assets are referred to as everything that is owned by a person or a company, and this includes everything from equipment to securities and even money. It also includes real estate. In short, everything that is owned to the person or company is included in the assets. You will find the mention of assets in the net worth statement of an individual or the balance sheet of a company.

Bear Market – When the prices of stocks are falling in a market, then it is said to be a bear market.

Beta – The beta value can show a measure of the relationship between the movement of the market as a whole and the price of a stock.

Blue Chip Stocks – The stocks belonging to those national companies that are leading the market and are known for paying their dividends continually and also offer other investment qualities that are deemed to be strong are known as blue chip stocks.

Bonds – Bonds are issued by the government or a corporation in the form of promissory notes to the lenders, and they are usually valid over a very specific period of time, and they also have a very specific rate of interest.

Broker – The connection between the stock market and the investors is made by the broker, and you can call them registered investment advisors. When an investor is selling or purchasing securities, the broker does not own those securities. They simply mediate the transaction, and they also charge a commission for it.

Bull Market – When the prices of stocks are rising in a market, it is referred to as the bull market.

Capital – If you considered from the economic point of view, then capital can be referred to anything like factories, machinery, inventory, and so on – basically anything that will be used for the manufacture of other products. But for investors, when the word capital is used, it usually refers to cash and any other financial assets they have.

Commission – Whenever you go to a broker or an investment advisor, they are going to charge you a certain fee, which is referred to as the commission.

Common Stock – These are the securities in a company that will give you voting rights along with part ownership in a particular company. It is the preferred shareholders who are first paid their dividends, and then the common shareholders are paid. Even if you consider the line of creditors, then the common shareholders are last in line.

Delta – Delta is basically a ratio with the help of which you can analyze the price movement of an option in comparison with the price movement of the underlying interest. The range of delta values is usually from 0 to 1. Options that are deep-in-the-money usually have their values closer to 1.

Diversification – It is one of the most popular risk management strategies with the help of which you can minimize your investment risk by investing your money, not in one but different securities, and these securities should preferably belong to different companies, each of which represents a separate sector of the economy.

Dividend – The percentage of equity of the issuer that is paid to the shareholder directly is termed as a dividend. It is usually the preferred and common shares that get dividends. However, there is no legal obligation on the issuer regarding paying the common or preferred dividends.

Equities – These are the preferred and common stocks, and they represent that you possess or own a portion of the company that is represented by that particular stock.

ETF or Exchange-Traded Fund – With the help of this fund, you can utilize a single security to buy a bunch of stocks, and all of these stocks will be following a specific market index in terms of returns. In fact, these funds are said to be a special category of index mutual funds, but the only difference is that they are traded like a stock and are listed on the exchange.

Growth Stock – These are stocks of a company that have shown a growth rate that is more than the average value of the market as seen over the past few years, and the usual expectation is that these stocks will keep growing in the near future.

Hedge – This is a type of risk management strategy through which you can limit your loss in any type of investment, and for this, you have to offset your current position by making another transaction.

Margin Account – This is a special type of account that the client uses for buying a security by taking credit from the investment dealer.

Market – The market is where the sellers and buyers meet each other to exchange services and goods, and it is the market where you will understand how much a service or product is in demand.

Mutual Fund – This is a special type of fund that is managed by a person who is an expert in this field and has a lot of knowledge about investments in bonds, stocks, options, and other types of securities. You can buy these funds either directly from the company of the mutual fund or through your broker.

Portfolio – The different types of securities you own are listed in the portfolio, and these securities might not only be from different companies, but they can even be from different sectors.

Preferred Share – This is a particular type of share capital which gives the owners the right to get dividends before the holders of common shares and to a pre-determined value per share in case there is liquidation. The holders of preferred shares generally do not have voting rights.

Printed in Great Britain
by Amazon

57617958R00113